普通高等学校"十四五"规划外语类一流课程建设新形态精品教材
省级一流课程"走进中美文化"配套教材

大学跨文化英语阅读教程

主 编◎向 玉 方 菲
副主编◎王 晴 桂 翊 张美琴 张培芳
编 者（按姓氏拼音排列）
　　　　陈 静 付容容 李媛莹 刘学思
　　　　刘媛妃 石婷玉 吴翠霞

华中科技大学出版社
http://press.hust.edu.cn
中国·武汉

图书在版编目(CIP)数据

大学跨文化英语阅读教程/向玉,方菲主编. —武汉:华中科技大学出版社,2024.4
普通高等学校"十四五"规划外语类一流课程建设新形态精品教材
ISBN 978-7-5772-0292-1

Ⅰ.① 大… Ⅱ.① 向… ② 方… Ⅲ.① 英语-阅读教学-高等学校-教材 Ⅳ.① H319.37

中国国家版本馆 CIP 数据核字(2024)第 078467 号

大学跨文化英语阅读教程
Daxue Kuawenhua Yingyu Yuedu Jiaocheng

向玉 方菲 主编

策划编辑:肖丽华
责任编辑:刘　凯
封面设计:廖亚萍
版式设计:赵慧萍
责任校对:张汇娟
责任监印:周治超

出版发行:华中科技大学出版社(中国·武汉)　　电话:(027)81321913
　　　　　武汉市东湖新技术开发区华工科技园　　邮编:430223

录　　排:华中科技大学出版社美编室
印　　刷:武汉开心印印刷有限公司
开　　本:787mm×1092mm　1/16
印　　张:12.75
字　　数:380 千字
版　　次:2024 年 4 月第 1 版第 1 次印刷
定　　价:58.00 元

本书若有印装质量问题,请向出版社营销中心调换
全国免费服务热线:400-6679-118　竭诚为您服务
版权所有　侵权必究

Preface 前 言

一、教材定位

党的二十大报告强调了加快构建中国话语和中国叙事体系的重要性,倡导讲好中国故事、传播好中国声音,以展示一个可信、可爱、可敬的中国形象。高校肩负着重要的职责,包括人才培养、科学研究、社会服务、文化传承创新和国际交流合作等,拥有人才储备和学科积淀等独特优势,因此成为国际传播的重要力量。

根据《大学英语教学指南(2020版)》的指示,跨文化交际课程是大学英语教学的核心内容之一。这些课程的重点是展现大学英语的人文特性。各高校可以根据需求开设不同级别的跨文化交际课程,这些课程主要包括文化类和跨文化交际类,旨在帮助学生提高对文化和跨文化的认知,增强跨文化交际能力。

本教材是湖北工业大学省级线上线下混合式一流课程"走进中美文化"的配套教程。它的目标在于协助学生更好地理解和适应多元文化社会,拓展学生的跨文化视野,提升学生的跨文化沟通技巧,为他们未来的国际交流和职业发展奠定坚实基础。

二、内容简介

本教材包含10个单元,重点介绍了饮食、教育、节日、婚俗、音乐、交通、建筑、医疗、文学等经典的社会文化。在编写本教材的过程中,我们经过精心考究,力求选材合理、内容导向清晰、层次递进。我们的目标是帮助学习者拓宽国际视野,树立跨文化交际意识,并提升他们的英语综合运用能力、自主学习能力和批判性思维能力。

本教材不仅适用于高校英语文化类选修课,还可以作为英语专业本科教材,同时也可供英语文化爱好者阅读参考。此外,本教材还配备了线上资源,教师可以开展线上线下相结合的混合式教学实践。

三、教材特色

(1)兼顾中西文化,着眼对比交流。本教材编写充分考虑了学生跨文化交际能力的新要求,根据《大学英语教学指南(2020版)》和"中国大学生跨文化交际能力量表"的要求,旨

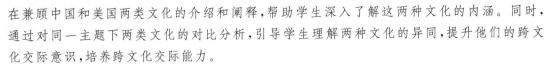

在兼顾中国和美国两类文化的介绍和阐释,帮助学生深入了解这两种文化的内涵。同时,通过对同一主题下两类文化的对比分析,引导学生理解两种文化的异同,提升他们的跨文化交际意识,培养跨文化交际能力。

(2)主题贴近生活,融合新兴话题。本教材精选了与学生生活密切相关的主题,如饮食、教育、节日和婚俗等,以及具有新时代特色的当代文化主题,如新能源、医疗等。我们的目标是既满足学科知识的学习需求,又培养学生的创新思维和解决实际问题的能力。通过对历史的借鉴,关注当下的发展,展望未来的趋势。我们希望学生能够更好地理解中国文化的博大精深,同时也能够应用所学知识解决实际问题。

(3)聚焦课程思政,培养文化自信。本教材将培养和提升政治认同、家国情怀、文化素养、道德修养和专业知识五个方面作为课文选材依据。通过文本阅读,我们引导学生坚守中华文化的立场,坚定文化自信;同时,加强对世界优秀文化的教育,尊重世界文化的多样性,培养学生融通中外的跨文化理解和跨文化传播能力。这有助于提高学生的语言能力、文化认知水平和跨文化交际能力,让他们在全球化的背景下更好地了解和融入世界。

(4)线上线下融合,创设互动情境。本教材的课文内容与线上资源高度匹配,我们提供了线上视频二维码,教材活动设计兼顾了线上学习的巩固和线下拓展与思考,积极适应线上线下混合式教学模式。此外,我们还为教师提供了案例库等多种教学活动的支持,以提升教学的针对性和有效性,使教学更具有交互性和参与性。

▼ 四、教材设计

本教材的设计充分结合了党的二十大报告,以引出各个单元的主题。同时,教材内容与线上视频内容高度协调,进一步丰富和深化了主题。我们的教材活动设计旨在同时满足线上学习的检测巩固以及线下拓展和思考的需求。

对于线上学习部分,我们精心设计了多种丰富的题型,包括词汇题、改错题、填词题、选择填空题和判断题,以帮助学生更好地掌握知识。此外,我们还根据思辨的六个维度设计问题,引导学生深入思考,为线下阅读提供了坚实的基础。

对于线下学习部分,我们特别设计了"Global Perspective"和"Case Study"。通过文化对比,我们旨在提高学生的跨文化意识;而通过案例研究,让学生在具体的文化情境中进行学习。这样的设计有助于学生更好地理解和应用所学知识。

通过本教材,我们期望能够为学生提供一个全面的跨文化学习体验,让他们在全球化的背景下更好地融入和参与国际社会,为中国的国际传播事业贡献自己的力量。

希望本教材成为学生提升跨文化交际能力的有效工具,也希望它为促进中国文化的传播和交流做出积极的贡献。我们期待学生通过学习本教材,培养更广阔的国际视野,拥有更强的跨文化交际技能,为建设一个更加开放和多元化的世界贡献自己的智慧和力量。

编　者
2023年10月

Contents 目 录

Unit 1 Food and Etiquette ······· **001**
  Section A ······· **002**
    Knowledge Focus ······· 002
    Language Focus ······· 005
    Critical Thinking ······· 006
    Case Study ······· 007
  Section B ······· **009**
    Passage 1   Chinese Medicinal Cuisine ······· 009
    Passage 2   American Fast Food Obsession ······· 013
  Cross-cultural Perspectives ······· **015**
    Case Study ······· 018

Unit 2 Education ······· **020**
  Section A ······· **021**
    Knowledge Focus ······· 021
    Language Focus ······· 025
    Critical Thinking ······· 026
    Case Study ······· 027
  Section B ······· **027**
    Passage 1   Education in China ······· 027
    Passage 2   In the Real World, Nobody Cares that You Went to an Ivy League School ······· 031
  Cross-cultural Perspectives ······· **035**
    Case Study ······· 037

Unit 3 Traffic and Transportation ······· **039**
  Section A ······· **040**
    Knowledge Focus ······· 040
    Language Focus ······· 044

Critical Thinking ·· 045
　　Case Study ·· 046
　Section B ··· 046
　　Passage 1　China's Unique Approach to Electric Vehicles ················ 046
　　Passage 2　The Price of Oil and the Price of Carbon ······················ 049
　Cross-cultural Perspectives ··· 053
　　Case Study ·· 056

Unit 4　Festivals and Celebrations ·· 058
　Section A ··· 059
　　Knowledge Focus ·· 059
　　Language Focus ·· 062
　　Critical Thinking ·· 064
　　Case Study ·· 064
　Section B ··· 065
　　Passage 1　A Guide to Traditional Chinese Festivals ······················ 065
　　Passage 2　April Fools' Day: What Are Its Origins and How Do Europeans
　　　　　　　Celebrate? ·· 069
　Cross-cultural Perspectives ··· 072
　　Case Study ·· 075

Unit 5　Wedding Customs and Ceremonies ······································ 076
　Section A ··· 077
　　Knowledge Focus ·· 077
　　Language Focus ·· 081
　　Critical Thinking ·· 082
　　Case Study ·· 083
　Section B ··· 083
　　Passage 1　Bride Price Tradition Fueling Fresh Friction ················ 083
　　Passage 2　Six Things to Ask Yourself before Getting Married ········ 087
　Cross-cultural Perspectives ··· 090
　　Case Study ·· 094

Unit 6　Music and Instruments ·· 095
　Section A ··· 096
　　Knowledge Focus ·· 096
　　Language Focus ·· 100

  Critical Thinking ··· 101
  Case Study ·· 102
 Section B ·· 102
  Passage 1 Chinese Music ·· 102
  Passage 2 A Brief Overview of the Origins and Advancement of American
       Music ·· 106
 Cross-cultural Perspectives ·· 110
  Case Study ·· 112

Unit 7 Architecture ·· 113
 Section A ·· 114
  Knowledge Focus ··· 114
  Language Focus ··· 117
  Critical Thinking ··· 119
  Case Study ·· 119
 Section B ·· 120
  Passage 1 10 Things We Can Learn from Chinese Architecture ················ 120
  Passage 2 France's Beloved Cathedral Only Minutes Away from Complete
       Destruction ·· 124
 Cross-cultural Perspectives ·· 127
  Case Study ·· 130

Unit 8 Medicine and Healthcare ··· 132
 Section A ·· 133
  Knowledge Focus ··· 133
  Language Focus ··· 137
  Critical Thinking ··· 138
  Case Study ·· 139
 Section B ·· 139
  Passage 1 An Overview of the Chinese Healthcare System ······················ 139
  Passage 2 Reform and Medical Costs ··· 143
 Cross-cultural Perspectives ·· 147
  Case Study ·· 149

Unit 9 Drinks in Leisure Time ··· 151
 Section A ·· 152
  Knowledge Focus ··· 152
  Language Focus ··· 155

Critical Thinking	157
Case Study	157
Section B	**158**
Passage 1　Tea Drinking in China	158
Passage 2　What Is an Americano? Is It Different from Regular American Coffee?	163
Cross-cultural Perspectives	**167**
Case Study	170

Unit 10　Literature ... 171

Section A	**172**
Knowledge Focus	172
Language Focus	175
Critical Thinking	177
Case Study	177
Section B	**178**
Passage 1　Modern Chinese Literature	178
Passage 2　American Fiction in the 20th Century	182
Cross-cultural Perspectives	**186**
Case Study	189

参考文献 ... **192**

Unit 1
Food and Etiquette

Unit Objectives

- To master words and expressions about food and etiquette in China and the West.
- To gain a general knowledge about the features of food culture in China and the West.
- To express opinions about the food and etiquette.
- To develop a sense of appreciation and confidence in Chinese food culture.

Read and Discuss

Read the following paragraph and discuss the following questions.

We must reinforce the foundations for food security on all fronts. We will ensure that both Party committees and governments assume responsibility for ensuring food security and that

China's total area of farmland does not fall below the red-line of 120 million hectares. We will work to gradually develop all permanent basic cropland into high-standard cropland. We will invigorate the seed industry, support the development of agricultural science, technology and equipment, and refine the mechanisms for ensuring the incomes of grain growers and for compensating major grain-producing areas. With these efforts, we will ensure that China's food supply remains firmly in its own hands. We will adopt an all-encompassing approach to food, develop protected agriculture, and build a diversified food supply system.

1. What is the significance of prioritizing and strengthening the agricultural sector and ensuring food security?
_____

2. What measures will be taken to ensure China's food security?
_____

3. Why should we build a diversified food supply system and how to achieve that?
_____

Section A

▼ Knowledge Focus

Ⅰ. Fill in the blanks based on your understanding of the online video lectures.

●●● *Table Manners* ●●●

Chinese eat from their rice bowls, holding them from underneath and close to their lips like cups. 1) _____ are used to pick up small pieces of food and to push the rice into your mouth. When 2) _____ yourself, food is placed directly in the bowl. On a Chinese dining table, plates are also used, but they are used for placing 3) _____.

Business travelers to China should learn beforehand how to use chopsticks because there are many chopsticks 4) _____. For instance, when putting them down, do not put them 5) _____ on top of the bowl or in the bowl. Instead, put the chopsticks on their holder or rest them 6) _____ on the plate. Sticking them straight up in a rice bowl is considered rude, because they resemble 7) _____ used in religious ceremonies or to 8) _____.

1-1
Table Manners
扫码观看视频

As a guest, leaving a full bowl of food is considered rude. It is considered rude in many foreign countries, including China, not to 9) _____ of every dish. Finishing all the food served to you, though, might also 10) _____ your host, because it can imply the host didn't provide enough food. Never take the last piece of any dish, instead showing respect by offering it to others.

Ⅱ. Choose the best answer to each of the following questions.

1. What do Chinese cuisine and its cooking process reflect according to traditional Chinese philosophy?
  A. Disharmony and imbalance in nature.
  B. The pursuit of wealth and power.
  C. The harmony and balance of nature.
  D. The eradication of diseases through food.

2. According to the saying from *Huang Di Nei Jing*, what do the five vegetables provide?
  A. Nourishment.
  B. Support.
  C. Enrichment.
  D. Filling.

3. What are the characteristics of Shandong cuisine?
  A. Wide selection of materials and use of diverse cooking methods.
  B. Distinct natural flavors in various ingredients.
  C. Use of fresh seafood and a wide variety of meat.
  D. Fresh and soft, with the flavor of mellow fragrance.

4. What does neutral food represent in Chinese food philosophy?
  A. Promoting yin in the human body.
  B. Promoting yang in the human body.
  C. A cold temperature in the human body.
  D. A balance of the human body.

5. How should guests seat themselves at a business dinner in China?
  A. According to their preference.
  B. Closest to the entrance.
  C. In descending order of importance.
  D. Next to the host.

6. Which of the following is NOT true about American food culture?
A. Diversity.
B. Integration.
C. Nutrition.
D. Migration.

7. In America, when will the local custom dictate the time of the lunch?
A. 1:30 P. M.
B. 1:00 P. M.
C. 11:30 A. M.
D. 2:00 P. M.

8. Which of the following is NOT considered a conversation stopper in America?
A. Religion.
B. Illness.
C. Travel.
D. Racial jokes.

9. What contributes to the uniqueness of American food?
A. Borrowing flavors from multiple cultures.
B. Strict preservation of traditional dishes.
C. Homogeneity within the cuisine.
D. Avoiding foreign influences.

10. How much personal space do Americans generally like to have after shaking hands?
A. Close proximity.
B. At least an arm's length away.
C. It varies depending on the person.
D. No personal space is preferred.

Ⅲ. Decide whether each of the following statements is true (T) or false (F).

1. In China, people usually accept an invitation to a business meal immediately.

2. In Chinese official business meetings, you will be offered a big hug.

3. Saying some favorable words to your business partner is an effective way to show your respect and sincerity in China.

4. In China, the most honored guest sits on the side of a table furthest away from the entrance.

5. In China, the host will generally sit in the middle of a round table.

6. In China, you should refill your own glass while drinking.

7. The person who initiates the dining usually foot the bill of the business dining in the United States.

8. Americans are straight forward and say what they mean.

9. Business cards should be handed out formally and kept with care in the United States.

10. The waiter or waitress usually gets 25% of the total bill before tax is added.

▽ Language Focus

Ⅰ. Match the words and definitions.

____ counterpart   ____ culinary   ____ diagonal   ____ eclectic
____ euphemistic   ____ indigenous   ____ ingredient   ____ infiltrate
____ reciprocate   ____ tangible

A. a person or thing that has the same position or function as somebody or something else in a different place or situation

B. that can be clearly seen to exist

C. to enter or make somebody enter a place or an organization secretly, especially in order to get information that can be used against it

D. to use polite words and expressions to avoid shocking or upsetting people

E. connected with cooking, esp., as a developed skill or art

F. one of the things from which something is made, especially one of the foods that are used together to make a particular dish

G. at an angle; joining two opposite sides of something at an angle

H. to behave or feel towards somebody in the same way as they behave or feel towards you

I. not following one style or set of ideas but choosing from or using a wide variety

J. belonging to a particular place rather than coming to it from somewhere else

II. There are 10 errors altogether in the following paragraph(s). The errors are: missing words, unnecessary words and wrong words. Please correct them as follows: for a missing word, mark its position with the symbol "∧" and write it; for an unnecessary word, cross it out with the symbol "\"; for a wrong word, underline it and write the correct word.

Americans are straightforwarded. They say what they mean, because "yes" means "yes", "no" means "no", and "maybe" is not a polite way to say "no"—until it does mean "maybe". Even though it is considered rudely to interrupt someone when they are speaking, it often happen in the United States. If you hesitate to gather your thought or to think things through, someone else may jump and start talking to finish your sentence, otherwise take things in a new direction. If you would like to make up a point, you can say, "excuse me" where there is a pause and you can then continue.

1. _____
2. _____
3. _____
4. _____
5. _____
6. _____
7. _____
8. _____
9. _____
10. _____

● Critical Thinking

Discuss the following questions in small groups and share your ideas in class.

1. What are some important cultural differences between China and the West that western business travelers should be aware of when dining with colleagues or clients?

2. How did American chains like Pizza Hut, KFC, and Starbucks achieve significant success in China?

3. How do the western fast-food brands affect the development of Chinese restaurants?

4. Culture and life are inseparable. How do lifestyles affect food culture in China and the West respectively?

5. Why is there a significant amount of research conducted on table manners in both China and the West?

6. In what other ways can we perceive the concept that "food serves as a gateway to experiencing cultural diversity"?

Case Study

Growing up in a household in Oxford, Dunlop dreamed of becoming a cook when she was little. However, her dream did not start to materialize until she came to Chengdu, capital of Sichuan province, as a university student in 1994. That was when she began learning local cooking skills at the Sichuan Higher Institute of Cuisine.

Always keeping a notebook on hand wherever she went, she wrote down the recipes of the dishes she tasted. Based on her knowledge of Sichuan cuisine, Dunlop published her first book, Sichuan Cookery, in 2001, which was hailed by the Observer Food Monthly as "one of the top 10 cookbooks of all time".

Since then, she has published four books about Sichuan cuisine, and one in 2016 about recipes from Jiangnan, called *Land of Fish and Rice*. Now, a Chinese version of *Land of Fish and Rice*, translated by He Yujia, is available. In the book, Dunlop displays her profound understanding of the food culture that runs deep in the blood of Chinese people.

Having studied Chinese food culture for nearly two decades, she regards the Jiangnan region as the heartland of the nation's gastronomy. "Although you have really interesting and delicious food all over China, in this region, particularly, people wrote about it and discussed it. Many of the old classic food books came from this region, for example. So, if you talk about gastronomy, and not just about good food, then Jiangnan is a really important region", she says.

Dunlop spent 10 years researching the book. The decisive moment was in 2008 when she went to Longjing Caotang, a restaurant in Hangzhou, Zhejiang province, where the whole approach to ingredients, seasoning, cooking and tradition was so moving and impressive that, at that moment, she decided to write a book about the region, she says.

By then, she had published three books about Sichuan and Hunan cuisine, both of which are famous for being stimulatingly spicy. But in Hangzhou and Yangzhou, she encountered food that was calm, peaceful, soothing and delicate.

To better understand the context of the food in Jiangnan, Dunlop started reading Chinese classics like *The Dream of the Red Chamber* which contained detailed descriptions of dishes eaten by literati and aristocratic families in ancient China. "Jiangnan food is connected with Chinese literature. Lots of dishes have quite literary names or stories behind them", she says.

As a result, when introducing food in the book, besides tracing the history of the dishes, she also tells stories like how Su Dongpo, a great poet during the Song Dynasty (960-1279), invented Dongpo Pork in the 11th century, or quotes his poem that praises delicious sea bass.

After collecting all the recipes, Dunlop tested them at her home in London to make sure they worked for people in the West. "What I want to do is to try to describe the recipes accurately. If I make a change, I explain it", she says.

In total, there are more than 160 recipes that cover the typical food and dishes that people in Jiangnan eat, either at a banquet or at home every day. However, because Jiangnan is a large region, it was not easy for her to decide which dishes should be presented in the limited number of pages.

"In the end, it's just a matter of personal choice and judgment", she says, adding that she wanted to include as many as possible of the really essential famous dishes like Dongpo Pork, Westlake vinegar fish, and lion-head meatballs, "the really classic dishes". "It's like trying to paint a picture of the region and show its many different sides, from the banquet to the street food", she says.

Please write an essay to illustrate the role of food culture in cross-cultural communication.

Section B

▼ Passage 1

••• *Chinese Medicinal Cuisine* •••

[A] Through 5,000 years of recorded history, the Chinese have developed an unequaled pharmacopoeia of food remedies and have turned this knowledge into a delicious cuisine that is simple to prepare. In Traditional Chinese Medicine (TCM), food is viewed as medicine and is used to nourish and harmonize the body, mind and spirit. All foods have a distinct energy and characteristic properties that either help to balance our bodies and make us healthy, or that create imbalances which ultimately result in sickness.

A brief history of medicinal cuisine

[B] In ancient China, when people were looking for food sources, they found many things that could be eaten or not, but had medical effects through practice. Medicine and diet had been linked for a long time. Before the Xia Dynasty, wine making began and was used in medicine. The condiments after this also are medicaments like the genus of ginger, cassia. Originating from "Medicine and food being of the same origin", Chinese medical cuisine formed after the Qin (221 BC-207 BC) and Han (202 BC-220 AD) Dynasties and flourished in the Ming (1368-1644) and Qing (1644-1911) Dynasties.

[C] The earliest extant Chinese dietary text is a chapter of Sun Simiao's *Prescriptions Worth a Thousand Gold* (千金方), which was completed in the 652AD during the Tang Dynasty. Sun's work contains the earliest known use of the term "food (or dietary) therapy". Sun stated that he wanted to present current knowledge about food so that people would first turn to food rather than drugs when suffering from an ailment.

[D] His chapter contains 154 entries divided into four sections— on fruits, vegetables, cereals and meat— in which Sun explains the properties of individual foodstuffs with concepts borrowed from the *Yellow Emperor's Inner Canon*: Qi, the viscera, and vital essence, as well as correspondences between the five phases, the "five flavors" (sour, bitter, sweet, pungent and salty), and the five grains. He also set a large number of "dietary interdictions", some based on calendrical notions (no water chestnuts in the 7th month), others on purported interactions between foods (no clear wine with horse meat) or between different flavors. Chinese understandings of the therapeutic effects of food were influential in East Asia.

Main tenets of Chinese medicinal cuisine

[E] One of the basic concepts of Chinese Medicinal Cuisine is "medicine and food share a common origin", so that food materials can therefore be used to prevent or treat medical disorders.

Heats

[F] Like medicinal drugs, food items are classified as "heating" or "cooling". In popular understanding, "heating" or "hot" food is typically "high-calorie, subjected to high heat in cooking, spicy or bitter, or 'hot' in color (red, orange)", and includes red meat, innards, baked and deep-fried goods, and alcohol. They are to be avoided in the summer and can be used to treat "cold" illnesses like excessive pallor, watery feces, fatigue, chills, and low body temperature caused by a number of possible causes, including anemia. Green vegetables are the most typical "cooling" or "cold" food, which is "low-calorie, watery, soothing or sour in taste, or 'cool' in color (whitish, green)". They are recommended for "hot" conditions: rashes, dryness or redness of skin, heart-burns, and other "symptoms similar to those of a burn", but also sore throat, swollen gums, and constipation.

Five flavors

[G] Each medicine or food item has one of five flavors: sour, sweet, bitter, pungent (or "acrid"), and salty. Besides describing the taste of food, each of these "flavors" purportedly has specific effects on particular viscera. The sour flavor, for instance, has "constriction and emollient effects" and "can control diarrhea and perspiration", whereas "bitter" food can "purge the heart 'fire', reduce excessive fluids, induce diarrhea, and reinforce the heart 'yin'".

Five classification

[H] According to the perceived nature of food, there are five classifications: han 寒 (cold/yin), liang 凉 (cool/yin), ping 平 (neutral), wen 温 (slightly warm/yang), and re 热 (hot/yang).

- Han food: watermelon, persimmon, melon (cantaloupe), bitter lotus, crab and most seafood, etc.
- Liang food: mung bean, bean curd, mushroom, eggplant, wax gourd, towel gourd, cucumber, duck, duck egg, etc.
- Ping food: rice, corn, red beans, black beans, peanuts, tomatoes, carrots, pork, beef, etc.
- Wen food: garlic, ginger, pumpkin, Chinese prickly ash, chicken, mutton, wine, beer, jujube, ginseng, etc.

• Re food: chili, pepper, cinnamon, white flour, soybean oil, white wine, etc.

General principles of Chinese medicinal cuisine

Balance

[I] The basic idea is to balance the Qi and the body fluids— the fundamentals of Chinese traditional medicine. It is thought that a healthy body or organ has a proper balance of these things. When they are out of balance, there is disease or sickness. The environment or physical injury disrupts the balance. For example, cold weather causes a lack of Qi or high yin in the body. So high yang foods are eaten. In hot weather when there is naturally too much yang, high yin foods are eaten.

Adding medicinal herbs

[J] Healing herbs or animal parts can be added to the diet to heal disease. Many of the same herbs are used by Western herbalists and herbalists in other parts of the world for the same conditions, so this strongly suggests that the herbs have real medicinal effects.

Using heats and flavors

[K] All foods are categorized by Qi temperature, ranging from high yang to high yin, and one of the five food flavors (sour, sweet, bitter, hot and salty). A food item's Qi temperature and specific flavor influences the body in its own way. It is thought that people should generally include all the flavors in every meal and balance the "heat". Most Chinese people think that if too much of one type of food is consumed, it can cause an imbalance in the body.

Mealtime principles

[L] The way you eat also matters. Eating slowly is believed to benefit your health. The ancient texts described not only what to prepare for meals, but also how to eat meals. You might be surprised at these Chinese customs about eating meals that have been part of the culture for hundreds of years.

• Try to avoid overly processed food. Eat naturally.

• Eat seasonal vegetables and fruits.

• Always make sure the vegetables are cooked.

• Sit down to eat at a quiet place.

• Chew the food well.

• Eat slowly.

• Pay attention to your eating, and get away from distractions. Your mind plays a part in how well you digest food, so pay attention to the tastes of the food.

• Do not skip meals.

• After lunch, take a nap or rest for a while.

Seasonal recipes help you live longer

[M] Chinese believe that eating seasonal food is generally best. For example, in summer yin foods like melons and cucumber are available, and in winter high yang foods like garlic and onions are available for consumption as well as easily stored red pepper and other high yang herbs. It is as if nature produces the right healing foods for each season for people.

[N] In the spring, things come alive and start growing. It is important for living things to have more than usual yang for growth. It is thought that the liver and gall bladder are especially important at this time. It is important to eat the green seasonal vegetables that sprout out at these times since they supply the necessary yang and help to nourish the liver. "Green is the color of the liver and of spring" is a saying. And drink fresh sour juices, since these stimulate the Qi.

I. Fast reading.

Direction: Each statement of the following contains information given in one of the paragraphs in the above passage. Identify the paragraph from which the information is derived. You may choose a paragraph more than once. Each paragraph is marked with a letter.

1. Different types of food have specific effects on the internal organs of the human body.

2. The concept of Qi was first mentioned in the *Yellow Emperor's Inner Canon*.

3. Green vegetables are considered cold food and are often recommended for individuals with hot conditions.

4. Chinese medical cuisine has developed more than one thousand years from Qin Dynasty.

5. Maintaining a balance between yin and yang is essential for overall health.

6. Slight warmth is one of the perceived qualities of certain foods.

7. Excessive consumption of salty food can lead to an imbalance in the body.

8. It is advisable to chew food thoroughly and eat slowly.

9. According to TCM, food provides nutrition but can also be used to treat diseases.

10. High yang herbs are much more popular among Chinese in cold days.

II. Translate the following paragraph into English.

中国传统的待客之道要求饭菜丰富多样,让客人吃不完。中国宴席上典型的菜单包括开席的一套凉菜及其后的热菜,例如,肉类、鸡鸭、蔬菜等。大多数宴席上,全鱼被认为是必不可少的,除非已经上过各式海鲜。如今,中国人喜欢把西方特色菜与传统中式菜肴融于一席,因此牛排上桌也不少见。沙拉也已流行起来,尽管传统上中国人一般不吃任何未经烹饪的菜肴。宴席通常至少有一道汤,可以最先上或最后上桌。甜点和水果通常标志宴席的结束。

Passage 2

American Fast Food Obsession

[1] Fast food is a presence in almost everybody's life on a daily basis. Over a quarter of American adults eat fast food daily.

[2] There are many factors that contribute to America's obsession with fast food. Fast food is extremely easy to obtain, in most cases you don't even need to leave the comfort of your car to enjoy a meal. Secondly, fast food is very cheap, a Big Mac meal from McDonald's costs only $5.99 and includes a burger, fries and a drink. Finally, getting a meal from a fast food restaurant is quick, in most cases your food will be prepared and served in well under 10 minutes. These factors are the main contributors to fast food's popularity in the United States and due to all of these factors, fast food in America has been on a steady increase for years and will not slow down anytime soon.

[3] One of the main reasons for fast food's popularity is the convenience factor. Instead of having to spend time in your kitchen and at a grocery store preparing a meal you can spend mere minutes at a fast food restaurant and get a full meal. McDonald's is the most popular fast food restaurant, with over 37,000 locations, it completely dwarfs all other fast food restaurants in number of locations. The way in which McDonald's serves their food is one important factor in its convenience. With most meals at McDonald's you don't need any kind of cutlery to eat your meal, just your hands will do. This means that their meals can be eaten anywhere at any time. Because of this, over 20% of American meals are eaten in cars, a concept that didn't exist before fast food. For many people time is a major factor in their decision on where and what to eat. For example, many college students find it hard to find time in their day to cook or go out and sit down for a healthy meal. Due to this it has been reported that 23% of college students eat fast food daily and 50% of students reported eating at least 3 fast food meals per week. Because of its convenience, fast food has a firm grip over a large part of the American food economy. It is viewed as quick and easy by many people and many people find those qualities attractive in their food. Fast food plays into this narrative and advertises it heavily in order to retain this portion of the market and therefore maintain its overwhelming presence in American society.

[4] One of the biggest contributing factors to fast food's vast presence in America is its low cost. The typical American spends $1,200 annually on fast food. With fast food meals being so cheap, this means that a person can stretch their dollar much further going to a fast food restaurant rather than preparing their own food or going out to eat at a traditional sit-down restaurant. Many people perceive fast food as the least expensive dining option available and therefore are drawn to it. The vast majority of fast food ads include their prices so people are ensured to know that the food not only looks appetizing but also won't hurt their bank account. In a survey, 32% percent of people stated that they ate fast food because it is cheap. Due to this perception, Americans spend over $50 billion annually on fast food. This staggeringly large number perfectly exemplifies the magnitude of the obsession that Americans have with fast food. When people know that they can get a full meal for well under $10, they are going to often take that option. Fast food companies have recognized this and tailored their marketing and pricing strategies to fit that mindset. Fast food and low prices go hand in hand and that is one of the major factors of why Americans choose to eat fast food so often.

[5] The final reason why fast food is so popular in America is because the time between placing your order and receiving your food is very short. The reason behind why fast food companies are able to churn out orders so quickly is because almost everything in the fast food process has become mechanized. Almost everything on the menu was mass produced in a factory somewhere and then frozen and shipped out to the thousands of nearby storefronts. This cuts down almost all the prep time that the "cooks" need so that your order will be prepared in mere minutes. Many people who feel that they don't have the time to get any other kind of meal will turn to fast food despite its negative health effects. A study of college students showed that 46% of fast food meals eaten were at lunch time. This statistic is important because lunch is a time in the middle of the day where people don't have a lot of time. The fact that many college students elected to eat fast food for lunch shows that they believe fast food is the quickest and therefore best option for their mid-day meal.

[6] How does fast food affect culture is something most people do not give much thought. However, they do and it is becoming a global issue.

[7] Before fast food restaurants, people had to prepare their own meals or go to an expensive restaurant. This meant that only people with excess amounts of money could afford to eat out. Once McDonald's began serving fast food, even poorer people could have the experience of eating out. Soon, other entrepreneurs were attempting to duplicate their success. Today, most fast food chains offer a dollar menu or other list of inexpensive items.

[8] How fast food affect culture for patrons is that they no longer have to be involved with their food preparation. So, people lose the opportunity to spend time with their family in the kitchen and to hand down family recipes. It also means that people expect whatever they want quickly.

[9] The ingredients in fast food are another concern. How fast food affects culture here is

that people do not know or think about what is in the food they eat. When people prepare their own meals, they consciously choose each ingredient and are more involved in ensuring that their family is eating a balanced diet. Fast food contains high levels of sugar, salt, fat, and preservatives. It is a great contributor to the obesity levels in America. As fast food chains expand to the global market, other countries are beginning to have similar problems.

[10] Unfortunately, poor health and a hurried lifestyle are by-products of the patrons of fast food restaurants. Until the chains make a choice to serve healthier selections, these problems are likely to grow.

I. **Answer the following questions.**

1. What are the main factors contributing to America's obsession with fast food?

2. How has fast food contributed to a change in American dining habits?

3. Why is fast food perceived as the least expensive dining option available?

4. How does the mechanized process of fast food preparation contribute to its popularity?

5. Why is fast food becoming a global issue in terms of its impact on culture?

II. **Translate the following paragraph into Chinese.**

As a country gets richer, it invests more and more in getting more and more surplus into its shops and restaurants, and as you can see, most European and North American countries fall between 150 and 200 percent of the nutritional requirements of their populations. So a country like America has twice as much food on its shop shelves and in its restaurants than is actually required to feed the American people.

Cross-cultural Perspectives

Read the following paragraph and write a summary of 200 words.

••• *Is Food a (Cross-Cultural/Interpersonal) Communication Medium?* •••

Identity & Food

[1] The brain consumes more energy than any organ in the human body, about 25% of the

total energy. One of the brain's most important tasks is finding nutritious food. In the case of human beings, the brain uses all the senses, but mainly vision, to look for food. "The fact that the brain and the mouth are both at the same end of the body may not be as trivial as it seems." Food has an existential importance for the brain. On the other hand, the brain is the same organ, which defines our behavior, reflects on its own activities, stores memories and controls emotions. The brain is the one who defines who we are and develops the concept of "self" and identity. Probably that is why there is such a strong visceral link between identity and food. The emotions and memories have a big influence on that link.

[2] People use food as a means to express their identity to others as well as identify themselves with others. Food and the traditions around it, carry historical identities, which can be used to communicate about the identity of a community. It functions as a cultural memory. "It is symbolically associated with the most deeply felt human experiences, and thus expresses things that are sometimes difficult to articulate in everyday language." Food is used as a sign of national and regional identity. Feta cheese for the Greeks, champagne for the French, Parmigiano-Reggiano for the Italians, and endless other examples are more than just food for people from those geographical locations. The Turkish and the Greeks still argue about whose baklava is the original one. Iran and Turkey are competing to register pomegranate as their own national fruit.

[3] Thus, food in different contexts works as an identity marker. Food can indicate the income level, wealth and social class of people. For instance, caviar is a symbol of the most luxurious and expensive food. Eating caviar sends a clear message about the diner's status. If someone eats caviar but does not know how to handle it or which drink should be drank with it, it will send a totally different kind of message. Equally, in social terms, food indicates different aspects of identity such as religion, gender, age, political preferences, etc.

[4] Food exhibits relationships between individuals and groups. "Social relationships are developed and maintained by symbols and, thus, we tend to see groups through their symbols and to identify ourselves through symbols." Eating a particular food can indicate group affiliation

while eating the other group's food can be considered as a sign of accepting them. For example, a majority group eating food of an ethnical minority group sends a message of acceptance in the wider majority group. By ingesting the foods of each new group, people symbolize the acceptance of each group and its culture.

[5] In the Iranian culture having someone's salt and bread is a sign of loyalty to that person. Nobody literally offers salt and bread to each other, but the concept strongly remains in the daily life of Iranians. The intrapersonal and interpersonal function of food connects people psychologically, physically, socially and symbolically to each other. It would be enough to remind someone that you already had his/her salt and bread to bring peace of mind that you are trusted. This study is an initiative to discover the "salt and bread" of different cultures and translate them into an international nonverbal language, which goes beyond linguistic and cultural barriers.

Time & Food

[6] Is it possible to communicate an abstract concept such as time by means of food?

[7] The transitory nature of food is one of its fundamental characteristics. Food on a photo frame is captured, stopped and stored forever, but food itself is not a static artifact. The moment that food is ready, its spoiling process has started. Food grows from the ground, gets mature and gradually goes back to the ground. It would be called food if someone eats it between those two moments. Food is dynamic. Time shapes and reshapes food. Time is an inseparable element of food. If the element of time is extracted from food, it will turn into a still-life photo.

[8] A piece of fresh meat at room temperature will change its message. The message might get old and out of date or transform to something new: rotten meat or aged meat. However, time does not necessarily always have a negative impact on food. Cooking is a time-consuming process; fruits need time to ripen and cheese and wine get mature by time. Even freezing food just slows down the process of spoiling, but it does not stop it. There are other culinary techniques which manipulate the effect of time on food, such as pickling, drying, saturating in sugar or salt, fermenting etc.

[9] Time is controlled in every kitchen. Time is part of the food during the preparation process, serving, consumption and storage. Freshness, temperature, mold, steam, crunchiness of herbs and so on are all indicators of time in food. Flavor can indicate time too; such is the case of, for example, sour milk. Sound can indicate time in food; ripen watermelon sounds more bass compared to unripe one. Obviously food is a four dimensional phenomena. All those are possibilities in the hands of chefs and food designers to communicate time by food.

[10] These examples about the influence of time on food remind of the culinary triangle of Claude Lévi-Strauss. He approached cuisine (as part of a culture) as he did with a language to identify a binary system of the opposite terms and concepts. He believed that those binary sets would provide details about the social structure of different cultures. He draws the culinary

triangle based on the culinary methods and practices, which are employed to prepare food to argue that they express the mental structure of human beings. The presence of the concept of time in the triangle is obvious although it has not been mentioned. Time is one of the elements that cause the contrast between each couple of the corners of the triangle. Temperature or bacteria need a certain amount of time to transform a raw material to cooked or rotten one.

[11] It is possible to communicate dates and seasons too by food. Festive foods in their cultural context indicate a particular time of the year. For instance, mämmi is a sign of Easter in the Finnish context, while its Iranian cousin, samanu, indicates the beginning of the Iranian New Year. Both also remind people of the beginning of spring. Food can point out a historical occasion too. Therefore, there are endless opportunities in food for communicating a complex and abstract idea such as time.

▼ Case Study

Asian food lovers are fuming over a video that they say "manhandles" traditional soup dumplings. The video published by Time Out London on Facebook shows diners attempting to burst their Xiao Long Bao (little basket buns), and throw out the soup. The video has been widely panned by food lovers on Facebook, many of whom criticized the "lack of education" that went into filming. In order to appease foodies' anger, Time Out London expressed its apology in a passage as follows.

After our recent video on Chinese dumplings, we've been politely informed that bursting these lovely little parcels of culinary joy before they reach your lips really isn't the done thing at all.

So, first off, apologies to anybody who was peeved by our post. Secondly, we'd like to invite the knowledgeable food-lovers of China and the rest of Asia to tell us what traditional delicacies Londoners should try and how to eat them properly. We're an inquisitive bunch at heart you know, and while we don't always do things the traditional way, we're always looking to learn.

Work collaboratively in groups to produce a 5-minute video illustrating your comprehension of this "soup dumpling" event that exemplify the cultural disparities between Eastern and Western food culture.

1-2　Unit 1 译文及答案

Unit 2 Education

Unit Objectives

- To master words and expressions about education in China and the West.
- To gain a general knowledge on the features of education in China and the West.
- To express informed opinions and thoughtful analysis about education.
- To foster a positive perception of Chinese education and its contribution to personal growth and societal development.

Read and Discuss

Read the following paragraph and discuss the following questions.

Education is of critical importance to the future of our country and our Party. What kind of people we should cultivate, how, and for whom these are the fundamental issues that education must address. The most basic aim of education is to foster virtue. We will fully implement the Party's educational policy, carry out the basic task of fostering virtue through education, and nurture a new generation of capable young people with sound and moral grounding, intellectual ability, physical vigor, aesthetic sensibility, and work skills who will fully develop socialism and carry forward the socialist cause. We will continue to follow a people-centered approach to developing education, move faster to build a high-quality educational system, advance students' well-rounded development, and promote fairness in education.

1. What are the fundamental issues that education must address, and why are these issues considered crucial?

_____

2. How does the Party plan to nurture a new generation of capable young people?

_____

3. What is your perspective on the significance of nurturing talents?

_____

Section A

▼ Knowledge Focus

Ⅰ. **Fill in the blanks based on your understanding of the online video lectures.**

••• *Famous Universities in China* •••

In October 2009, the first nine "985 Project" universities signed the Agreement of Top Universities on Cooperation and Exchange in 1)_____ under the principle of "complementing each other and sharing resources". That event marked the birth of the 2)_____ of nine prestigious universities (referred to as the C9), which is said to "have a significant influence on the development of Chinese higher education". On October 13 of that year, "the Chinese 3)_____ of the 'Ivy League'" was

2-1
Famous Universities
in China
扫码观看视频

added as the entry "C9" in the Baidu Encyclopedia. A spokesperson for the Ministry of Education delivered the clear support of the Ministry of Education for this coalition.

In September 2017, the Chinese Ministry of Education, Ministry of Finance and National Development and Reform Commission 4) _____ the detailed lists of universities and disciplines to be developed under 5) _____. The Double First-Class initiative is China's largest education development 6) _____ to date, aimed at increasing the global 7) _____ of China's university system by 2049 (the 100 year anniversary of the establishment of the People's Republic of China).

Under this initiative, 42 universities have been 8) _____ as having the potential to develop as world class, including 36 universities 9) _____ as type A (already well on the way to be world class) and 6 universities as type B (considered to have the potential to be world class). In addition, 465 disciplines from 140 universities (including the group of 42) are also identified as having the 10) _____ to become world class.

II. Choose the best answer to each of the following questions.

1. Which of the following is Not one of the Four Books of ancient Chinese education?

    A. *The Great Learning*.

    B. *The Doctrine of the Mean*.

    C. *The Analects of Confucius*.

    D. *The Book of Songs*.

2. Which of the following academy is particularly associated with the origin of Hunan University?

    A. Yuelu Academy in Changsha.

    B. Bailudong Academy on Mount Lushan.

    C. Songyang Academy in Dengfeng.

    D. Yingtian Academy in Shangqiu.

3. What type of writing style was required in the imperial civil examinations during the Ming and Qing Dynasties?

    A. Informal and creative writing.

    B. Poetry and calligraphy.

    C. Stereotyped Writing.

    D. Fictional storytelling.

4. What is the "double reduction" education policy issued by China?

    A. Reducing the duration of compulsory education.

    B. Reducing students' homework and after-school tutoring pressure.

C. Reducing the number of school subjects and exams students need to take.

D. Reducing the number of administrative staff in schools.

5. What is the aim of the Double First-Class initiative?

A. To increase the global recognition of China's university system by 2049.

B. To promote Chinese culture worldwide.

C. To become the top university system in the world by 2025.

D. To provide free education to all Chinese citizens.

6. Which of the following statements about the Ivy League is NOT true?

A. Ivy League schools are the most prestigious of all colleges in the United States.

B. Ivy League schools are the most sought-after in terms of acceptance and graduation.

C. All the eight schools were founded during the United States colonial period.

D. All the eight schools are private and extremely costly.

7. Which of the following is NOT generally considered in the admission standards for American graduate studies?

A. A statement of academic purpose.

B. Results from IQ tests.

C. Letters of recommendation.

D. Results from standardized tests.

8. Why do many students in the United States take the SAT or ACT?

A. To earn a high school diploma.

B. To improve their GPA.

C. To determine their next step into work or college.

D. To determine students' eligibility for scholarships.

9. What is encouraged in American classrooms, apart from independent thought?

A. Collaboration and participation.

B. Listening without question.

C. Silence during lectures.

D. Memorization of facts and figures.

10. How do professors usually manage students' participation in larger classes?

A. They ask students to raise their hands and wait to be called on before speaking.

B. They allow students to discuss freely without waiting for permission to speak.

C. They encourage students to only listen and not participate in class discussions.

D. They call on students randomly without any prior notice.

III. Decide whether each of the following statements is true (T) or false (F).

1. Private schools in ancient China had set textbooks and specified time span of study.

2. The Five Classics refer to *The Book of Songs*, *The Book of History*, *The Book of Rites*, *The Book of Changes*, and *The Spring and Autumn Annals*.

3. The imperial civil examination system was abolished in 1905 due to the spread of Western ideology and technology in China.

4. The law of compulsory education in China requires each child to have six years of formal education in primary school and three years in senior high school.

5. The "3+1+2" program in Gaokao reforms means students have to take three compulsory tests, one quasi-elective test, and two elective tests.

6. Western universities have shown no interest in accepting Gaokao scores as part of their international student application process.

7. Academic excellence, research ability and potential and good communication, interpersonal relationship, and leadership abilities are important factors for admission to graduate programs in China.

8. Colleges and universities in the U. S. only consider a student's high school GPA and diploma when making admissions decisions.

9. American private schools are locally controlled, because many states also set educational standards for them.

10. To receive a doctoral degree, candidates must pass a comprehensive examination.

Language Focus

I. Match the words and definitions.

____ adherence ____ conducive ____ connotation ____ consecutive
____ empower ____ encompass ____ inherent ____ nominate
____ prevail ____ residency

A. making it easy, possible or likely for something to happen

B. following one after another in a series, without interruption

C. to include a large number or range of things

D. to formally suggest that somebody should be chosen for an important role, prize, position, etc.

E. to give somebody the power or authority to do something

F. existing as a basic or permanent part of somebody/something and cannot be removed

G. to exist or be very common at a particular time or in a particular place

H. a house, especially a large or impressive one

I. an idea suggested by a word in addition to its main meaning

J. the fact of behaving according to a particular rule, etc., or of following a particular set of beliefs, or a fixed way of doing something

II. There are 10 errors altogether in the following paragraph(s). The errors are: missing words, unnecessary words and wrong words. Please correct them as follows: for a missing word, mark its position with the symbol "∧" and write it; for an unnecessary word, cross it out with the symbol "\"; for a wrong word, underline it and write the correct word.

In the United States, university classroom culture is student-focused. Classes tend to be learner-center, meaning that professors expect you cooperate and interact as part of the learning	1. _____ 2. _____

· 025 ·

experience. They may use several different teaching methods included lectures, group discussions, readings, projects, in-class assignments, and homework.

The relationship among college students and teachers tends to be formal. Professors may even ask you to call them by their first name. Teachers make time to work with students one-on-one. Most professors have office hours, are designated times when students can visit at the professor's office to ask question or get extra help with the course material.

In larger classes, professors may ask students to rise their hands and wait to be called on after speaking. In smaller classes, students may discuss free without waiting for permission to speak.

3. _____

4. _____

5. _____

6. _____

7. _____

8. _____

9. _____

10. _____

▼ Critical Thinking

Discuss the following questions in small groups and share your ideas in class.

1. What are some key cultural differences between the United States and China in terms of university classroom culture and how might these differences impact international students studying in the US?

2. What factors contribute to the consistently higher performance of Chinese students in standardized tests, such as the Program for International Student Assessment (PISA), compared to their American counterparts?

3. What are the potential benefits and drawbacks of the emphasis on rote memorization and exam-focused learning in the Chinese education system?

4. How might cultural exchange and globalization impact the future development of Chinese and American education?

5. How do cultural factors and societal expectations influence the differences observed in the education systems of China and the United States, such as the value placed on academic achievement or the role of parental involvement in education?

6. How do personal biases and cultural backgrounds influence our perception and understanding of Chinese and American education?

Case Study

Danna, a Chinese student enrolled in an American university, recently completed her first year in the US. Despite her proficiency in English, she faced challenges in the classroom due to her shyness. Danna found it difficult to speak up during class discussions. Observing her classmates engaging in lively debates, she anticipated her professor would invite her to share her opinions. However, she often felt too slow to contribute her views or make comments promptly. As the term concluded, Danna received lower scores than her classmates, partly due to her hesitancy to participate actively. This experience left her feeling disheartened because she believed she had diligently followed lectures and absorbed the course material.

As a student leader at Danna's university in the US, you have observed Danna's struggle to adapt to the new academic environment due to her shyness. Please write an email to help Danna overcome her challenges and thrive in her university studies abroad. In your letter, provide practical suggestions, encouragement, and resources that can assist Danna in building confidence, engaging in class discussions, and improving her academic performance.

Section B

Passage 1

Education in China

[1] China has the largest education system in the world. In June 2023, there were 12.91 million students taking the National Higher Education Entrance Examination (Gaokao) in China.

International students have enrolled in over 1000 higher education institutions throughout the country. Investment in education accounts for about 4% of total GDP in China. In 1986, the Chinese government passed a compulsory education law, making nine years of education mandatory for all Chinese children. Today, the Ministry of Education estimates that above 99 percent of the school-age children have received universal nine-year basic education.

[2] China has improved the quality of education through a major effort at school curriculum and other reforms. *China's Education Modernization* 2035 is launched to set the direction for the development of the education sector from "capacity" to "quality", and that the modernization of education should support the modernization of China.

[3] The Ministry of Education has launched a pilot education program which will allow 36 top universities in China including Peking, Tsinghua and Fudan University, to select outstanding high school graduates who are willing to serve the country's major strategic needs. Under the program, known as the Strong Base Plan, the universities will focus on enrollment in majors such as mathematics, physics, chemistry, biology that have been proved unpopular with students in recent years. Many students prefer to study in majors for high paying careers.

History of education in China

Confucianism

[4] Many Chinese scholars believe the history of education in China can be traced back at as far as the 16th century BC. Throughout this period of time, education was the privilege of the elites. During the Spring and Autumn and Warring States periods the teachings of Confucianism and the curriculum were mainly based on The Four Books and The Five Classics. The Four Books and The Five Classics were the acknowledged subjects of the Confucian culture in the feudal society in ancient China. The Four Books refers to *The Great Learning*, *The Doctrine of the Mean*, *Confucian Analects* and *The Works of Mencius*. And The Five Classics includes *The Book of Poetry* (also known as *The Book of Songs*, *The Book of Odes*), *The Book of History*, *The Book of Rites*, *The Book of Changes*, and *The Spring and Autumn Annals*.

[5] Confucianism probably is the biggest influence in education of China throughout the entire Chinese history. In Confucianism, a gentleman (Junzi) considers what is right, when the peasant considers what will pay. A gentleman trusts in justice and the peasant trusts in favor. A gentleman is generous and fair, when the peasant is biased and petty. A gentleman looks within for guidance and the peasant looks unto others. A gentleman is easy to serve, and hard to please. The peasant is hard to serve, and easy to please. A gentleman is to know what we know, and know what we do not know.

Civil Exam

[6] On the other hand, the common people should follow the traditions and rules. In ancient Chinese culture, there was no need for the common people to know why. For common

people, studying Confucianism and being a gentleman had been the most efficient way for them advancing into upper class. During Han Dynasty, the first civil service exam was set up. Confucianism, with no surprise, was one of the key subjects to study for the civil service exam. Provincial schools were established countrywide and the Confucianism tradition of education was spread all over China.

[7] "To enrich your family, there is no need to buy good land: Books hold a thousand measures of grain. For an easy life, there is no need to build mansion: In books are found houses of gold. When you go out, do not be upset if no one follows you: In books there will be a crowd of horses and carriages. If you wish to marry, don't be upset if you don't have a go-between: In books there are girls with faces like jade. A young man who wishes to be somebody will devote his time to the Classics. He will face the window and read." There were people who spend their entire lifetime studying on Confucianism in order to get respected, not only for themselves, but also for the pride of their family lines.

Project 211 and 985

[8] Project 211 is the Chinese government's new endeavor aimed at strengthening about 100 institutions of higher education and key disciplinary areas as a national priority for the 21st century. There are 112 universities in the project 211.

[9] The implementation of Project 211 is an important measure taken by the Chinese government in its effort to facilitate the development of higher education in the context of the country's advancement in social and economic fields. Primarily aiming at training high-level professional manpower to implement the national strategy for social and economic development, the project has great significance in improving higher education, accelerating the national economic progress, pushing forward the development of science, technology and culture, enhancing China's overall capacity and international competitiveness, and laying the foundation of training high-level professional manpower mainly within the educational institutions at home.

[10] Project 985 is a constructive project for founding world-class universities in the 21st century conducted by the government of the People's Republic of China. On May 4, 1998, then-President Jiang Zemin declared that "China must have a number of first-rate universities of international advanced level", so Project 985 was launched. In the initial phase, 9 universities were included in the project. The second phase, launched in 2004, expanded the program until it has now reached 39 universities.

Education system in China

Pre-school education in China

[11] Pre-school education is an important component of education cause in China. In urban areas, it is mainly kindergartens of 3 years, two years or one year which could be full time, part-time, boarding or hour-reckoned.

Primary and secondary education in China

[12] Since the promulgation of the "Compulsory Education Law of the People's Republic of China" in 1986, the 9-year compulsory education has been implemented by governments at various levels and made significant progress.

[13] Nine-year compulsory education policy in China enables students over six years old nationwide to have free education at both primary schools (grade 1 to 6) and junior secondary schools (grade 7 to 9). The policy is funded by government, and the tuition is free. Schools still charge miscellaneous fees. Senior secondary school (grade 10 to 12) and college education are not compulsory and free in China.

Higher education in China

[14] Since the implementation of Reform and Opening-up, the reform and development of higher education have made significant achievements. A higher education system with various forms, which encompasses basically all branches of learning, combines both degree-education and non-degree education and integrates college education, undergraduate education and graduate education, has taken shape. Higher education in China has played an important role in the economic construction, science progress and social development by bringing up large scale of advanced talents and experts for the construction of socialist modernization.

China's Education Modernization 2035

[15] The 2035 plan sets the goals of establishing a modern education system of lifelong learning, with universal quality pre-school education, balanced compulsory education, as well as enhanced vocational education and more competitive higher education. Education for those with disabilities should also be improved, so that the education system better serves the whole society.

[16] The 2035 plan includes eight goals: 1) virtue; 2) overall development; 3) people-orientation; 4) lifelong learning; 5) personalized teaching; 6) integration of knowledge and practice; 7) integrated development; 8) co-construction and sharing.

[17] In order to achieve these goals, the 2035 plan identifies several tasks including: improving teacher quality and the education infrastructure (laws, policies, qualifications framework, evaluation and assessment), reducing disparity and universalizing access to education, promoting life-long learning, and modernizing all education sectors with a particular focus on pre-school and vocational education and training.

[18] The implementation plan sets out actions for achieving those tasks, including in areas that have been prioritized in other national strategies, for example, the integration of industry in vocational education in the "Implementation Plan on National Vocational Education Reform", the "Belt and Road Initiative Education Action Plan", and mid-west region development promoted in plans like "The State Council General Office Guiding Opinions on Accelerating the Development of Education in the Midwest" and "Midwest Higher Education Promotion Plan".

[19] Under the implementation plan, a comprehensive evaluation system will be developed for the "Double First Class" Initiative. China will also implement several projects in higher education, targeting disciplines development, entrepreneurship, employment for undergraduates, and research and academic development for postgraduates.

[20] Also under the implementation plan, China seeks more efficiency and transparency in the management of Sino-foreign joint ventures and to optimize the distribution of Confucius Institutes and better promote Chinese language learning. International collaboration goals appear to be heavily focused on the "Belt and Road Initiative".

Ⅰ. **Reading comprehension.**

1. What is the purpose of China's pilot education program called the Strong Base Plan?

2. How did Confucianism influence education and social status in ancient China?

3. What are the broader implications of Project 211 and Project 985 on China's higher education landscape and international competitiveness?

4. What role has higher education played in China's development, as mentioned in the passage?

5. What projects will be implemented in higher education according to the implementation plan of the 2035 plan?

Ⅱ. **Translate the following paragraph into English.**

家庭教育问题自古以来就是人们关注的焦点,但被作为一种学科进行研究,在我国也只是近年来的事情。这是时代发展、人才需求、国民整体素质提高所必须涉及的问题。有人曾把儿童比作一块大理石,说把这块大理石塑造成一座雕像需要六位"雕塑家":① 家庭;② 学校;③ 儿童所在的集体;④ 儿童本人;⑤ 书籍;⑥ 偶然出现的因素。从排列顺序上看,家庭位列首位,可以看得出家庭在塑造儿童的过程中起到很重要的作用。

Passage 2

In the Real World, Nobody Cares that You Went to an Ivy League School

[A] As a high school junior, everything in my life revolved around getting into the right college. I diligently attended my SAT, ACT, and Advanced Placement test preparation courses.

I juggled cross-country and track schedules, newspaper staff, and my church's youth group and drama team. I didn't drink, party, or even do much dating. The right college, I thought, was one with prestige, one with a name. It didn't have to be the Ivy League, but it needed to be a "top school".

[B] Looking back now, nine years later, I can't remember exactly what it was about these universities that made them seem so much better. Was it a curriculum that appeared more rigorous, perhaps? Or an alumni network that I hoped would open doors down the line? Maybe. "I do think there are advantages to schools with more recognition," notes Marybeth Gasman, a professor of higher education at the University of Pennsylvania, "I don't necessarily think that's a reason to go to one."

[C] In reflection, my firm belief in the power of the brand was naive, not to mention a bit snobby. I quickly passed over state schools and southern schools, believing their curriculums to be automatically inferior to northeastern or western counterparts. Instead, I dreamed of living in New York City and my parents obliged me with a visit to New York University's (NYU) campus. During the tour, tuition fees were discussed. (NYU is consistently ranked one of the country's most expensive schools, with room and board costs totaling upwards of $64,000 a year.) Up until then, I hadn't truly realized just how expensive an education can be. Over the next few months, I realized not only could I not afford my dream school, I couldn't even afford the ones where I'd been accepted. City University of New York (CUNY), Rutgers University, and Indiana University were out of reach as were Mississippi State and the University of Alabama, where I would have to pay out-of-state fees. Further complicating my college search was a flourishing track career— I wanted to keep running but my times weren't quite fast enough to secure a scholarship.

[D] And so, at 11 p.m. on the night of Georgia State University's (GSU) midnight deadline, I applied online. Rated No. 466 overall on Forbes' Lists Top Colleges, No. 183 in Research Universities, and No. 108 in the South, I can't say it was my top choice. Still, the track coach had offered me a walk-on spot, and I actually found the urban Atlanta campus a decent consolation prize after New York City.

[E] While it may have been practical, it wasn't prestigious. But here's the thing: I loved my "lower-tier" university. (I use the term "low-tier" cautiously, because GSU is a well-regarded research institution that attracts high quality professors and faculty from all over the country.) We are taught to believe that only by going to the best schools and getting the best grades can we escape the rat race and build a better future. But what if lower-tier colleges and universities were the ticket to escaping the rat race? After all, where else can you leave school with a decent degree— but without a lifetime of debt?

[F] My school didn't come prepackaged like the more popular options, so we were left to take care of ourselves, figuring out city life and trying to complete degree programs that no one was championing for us to succeed in. What I'm saying is, I loved my university because it taught us all to be resourceful and we could make what we wanted out of it.

[G] I was lucky enough to have my tuition covered by a lottery-funded scholarship called HOPE (Helping Outstanding Pupils Educationally). When I started college, the HOPE scholarship was funded by the state of Georgia and offered to graduating high school seniors with a GPA of 3 or higher. Living costs and books I paid for with money earned during high school, supplemented by a small college fund my deceased grandfather left for me and a modest savings account my parents created when I was born.

[H] So what about all that name recognition? Sure, many of my colleagues and competitors have more glamorous alma maters (母校) than I do. As a journalist, I have competed against NYU, Columbia, and Northeastern graduates for jobs. And yet, not a single interviewer has ever asked me about my educational background. In fact, almost every interview I've ever had was due to a connection—one that I've gained through pure determination, not a school brand.

[I] According to *The Boston Globe*, students who earned their bachelor's in 2012 have an average monthly loan payment of $312, which is one-third more than those who graduated in 2004. Ultimately, that's the thing universities don't want to admit. Private universities are money-making institutions. If you can afford to buy prestige, that's your choice. For the rest of us, however, our hearty lower-tiered universities are just fine, thank you.

[J] Wealthy universities talk up the benefits their name will give graduates: namely, strong alumni networks, star faculty, and a résumé boost. But you needn't attend an Ivy League school to reap those rewards. Ludacris and the former CEO of Bank of America Ken Lewis are alumni of my college, as well as VICE's first female editor-in-chief, Ellis Jones. Successful people tend to be successful no matter where they go to school, and lower-tier schools can have alumni networks just as strong as their big name counterparts. In fact, lower-tier school alumni networks are arguably stronger, because fellow alumni recognize that you didn't necessarily have an easy path to follow. They might be more willing to offer career help, because your less famous school denotes that, like them, you are also full of energy and perseverance.

[K] *The Washington Post* reported on a recent study by Princeton economists, in which college graduates who applied to the most selective schools in the 12th grade were compared to those who applied to slightly less selective schools. They found that students with more potential earned more as adults, and the reverse held true as well, no matter where they went to school.

[L] Likewise, star faculties are not always found where you'd expect. Big name schools are not necessarily the best places for professors; plus, many professors split teaching time between multiple colleges and/or universities. This means, for instance, a CUNY student could reasonably expect to receive the same quality of instruction from a prestigious professor as they would if they were enrolled in the same class at NYU.

[M] It's possible that some hiring managers may be drawn to candidates with a particular educational résumé, but it's no guarantee. According to a 2012 survey described in *The Atlantic*, college reputation ranked lowest in relative importance of attributes in evaluating graduates for hire, beaten out by top factors like internships, employment during college, college major, volunteer experience, and extracurriculars.

[N] Maybe students who choose less prestigious universities are bound to succeed because they are determined to. I tend to think so. In any case, if I could do it again, I'd still make the same choice. Today I'm debt-free, resourceful and I understand that even the shiniest packaging can't predict what you'll find on the inside.

Ⅰ. **Fast reading.**

Direction: Each statement of the following contains information given in one of the paragraphs in the above passage. Identify the paragraph from which the information is derived. You may choose a paragraph more than once. Each paragraph is marked with a letter.

1. Modest institutions can also have successful graduates and strong alumni networks.

2. The money the author made in high school helped pay for her living expenses and books at college.

3. The author came to see how costly college education could be when she was trying to choose a university to attend.

4. A recent study found that a graduate's salary is determined by their potential, not the university they attended.

5. The author cannot recall for sure what made certain top universities appear a lot better.

6. None of the author's job interviewers cared which college she went to.

7. The author thought she did the right thing in choosing a less prestigious university.

8. In order to be admitted to a prestigious university, the author took part in various extracurricular activities and attended test preparation courses.

9. The author liked her university which was not prestigious but less expensive.

10. Colleges are reluctant to admit that graduates today are in heavier debt.

II. **Translate the following paragraph into Chinese.**

Cultivating as much talents as possible, getting as many girls as we can from all over into science and engineering, as many boys as we can into teaching—those are investments for our future. Our students are like our most valuable resource, and when you put it that way, our teachers are like our modern-day diamond and gold miners, hoping to help make them shine. Let's contribute our voices, our votes and our support to giving them the resources that they will need not just to survive but hopefully thrive, allowing all of us to do so as well.

Cross-cultural Perspectives

Read the following paragraph and write a summary of 200 words.

●●● *Education in Asia vs. the West: What's the Difference?* ●●●

[1] Some people have always stereotyped the Asian kid in class as the nerd or math wizard. Even in the media, Asian people are often depicted as super smart and geeky. And without actually knowing how the Asian education system works, Westerners assume that it's tougher on mathematics, sciences, and history.

[2] It is generally believed that the Western educational system is more creative and forward-thinking than that of Asia. True enough, anyone who's studying in Asia will agree that their schools are more conservative and reserved. For one thing, school uniforms are required, even in public schools. There are restrictions on haircuts and grooming as well.

[3] That said, many people also assume that Asian students are more disciplined and more likely to succeed later in life than their Western counterparts. Interestingly, international test trends show that Western students are lagging behind their Singaporean and Japanese peers.

Moreover, a 15-year-old from Shanghai made headlines after scoring first in the Program for International Student Assessment (PISA) in 2009.

[4] So, is it true, after all, that Asian schools produce smarter kids?

The differences in teaching style

[5] In Asia, the education system stresses more on the input from teachers. They are expected to rule the classroom, and students must listen to them with barely any interaction. A typical Asian class has a teacher providing all the study materials and students receive these materials without discussing them with their classmates.

[6] On the contrary, the Western education system is student-centered. It allows interaction between classmates, in the form of a group discussion or other types of engaging activities.

[7] With regard to teaching concepts, the Asian way is to have students memorize information. Teachers expect students to read their textbooks and memorize their contents so that they can answer their tests correctly. On the other hand, the Western way is more relaxed. Rather than memorizing information, teachers let students take their time in learning a concept. They require students to do their own research and share their personal views, instead of simply accepting what's written in textbooks.

Differences in school year and terms

[8] In China, the school year opens at the beginning of September and closes in mid-July. The average school day runs from 7:30 in the morning to 5 in the afternoon. Lunch break lasts for two hours. During the summer break, students are usually studying for their entrance exams or taking summer classes.

[9] Japan is different. The country's school year begins in April and ends in March. There are summer, spring, and winter breaks, dividing the school year into three trimesters.

[10] The Philippines had a different school year before the implementation of the K-12 system. The term used to start in June, and end in March. Some schools still maintain it, but many have already shifted to the September-to-July school year.

[11] In the U.S., the school year also starts in September and ends in May or June. Most schools have two semesters, but some use a quarterly term. A school day in elementary and high school usually runs from 8 A.M. to 3 or 3:30 P.M., with one hour of lunch. High school students take six 1-hour subjects and four 90-minute subjects.

Differences in results

[12] The teaching tactics in Asian schools may suffer disapproval from the West, but statistical data show shocking results. Students from Asian schools turn out to have higher standardized testing scores than their Western counterparts. Their math and science subjects are

more advanced than those in Western schools. In fact, American students lag behind 31 countries in math, and behind 16 countries in reading proficiency.

[13] Despite its strict nature, the Asian education system is earning favor from some Western countries, particularly the UK. In 2016, the UK Schools Standards Minister revealed that many primary schools in the country would use the teaching style used by the Chinese.

[14] But on the flip side, the Chinese seem impressed by the English-style of teaching, too. In 2016, Wymcobe Abbey opened a sister school in Changzhou Province. Harrow, Dulwich College, Malvern, and Wellington already opened branches in China's major cities, too, such as Beijing, Shanghai, and Chengdu.

[15] It's still unwise to conclude that one system is better than the other, though. In some Southeast Asian countries, low-quality education is a persistent national issue. In 2017, UNESCO asserted that Thai governments have failed to provide access to basic education. Meanwhile, in Cambodia and Laos, only 67% and 77% of students reach the last grade in secondary education, respectively.

[16] Therefore, when choosing where to study, be it for college, vocational, or postgraduate degree, avoid making judgments based on the school's country or location alone. For instance, if you want to enroll in a traineeship program in Singapore, do it because the program is exceptional, not because you believe that Asia is superior to the West.

[17] If it's unethical to stereotype people based on their race, then it's also unethical to judge schools based on their location. So, despite the vast differences between the Asian and Western education systems, both produce smart, competent, and successful students.

▼ Case Study

It is not an uncommon belief that Chinese students are smarter than their American counterparts. Education experts, psychologists, and scientists have hypothesized and studied why Chinese students often outperform American students. Part of the answer lies in the foundational beliefs about the purpose of education.

In China, learning aims to accumulate knowledge. Chinese students are taught from the age of 2-3 years that learning is critical to success, and that discipline and strictness are required in that pursuit. There is a high focus on memorization and a fundamental understanding of calculations— Chinese students are not even allowed to use calculators.

American education, on the other hand, focuses more on creativity and how the students will use the knowledge in society. Homework is not just memorizing facts and demonstrating skills, but applying originality to the work in the form of critiquing thoughts and challenging the status quo.

Chinese students stay with the same two or three teachers all the way through elementary school and into primary school, and the teachers are responsible for groups of 40 or more students. The Chinese teacher thinks, "How can I help this group the most?" Homework is assigned every day, with assignments over all of the holidays and breaks, and there is strong pressure to perform well on end of year exams.

In contrast, American teachers are encouraged to focus on individual students, creating plans like Individual Education Plans to structure a subject to a specific student's learning needs. The American teacher thinks, "How can I help this student the most?" Many schools have done away with homework altogether, whether because they think students don't need the extra practice or because students don't bother to do it. End of year exams are often viewed as just another test to pass.

In Chinese society, there is a high value on learning and education for future success. Beginning in preschool, Chinese parents communicate early that their children are expected to succeed in school, which has a very competitive environment. Students do not typically have time for extra-curricular activities as the school day runs long and then they must complete homework.

American parents tend to view education and learning as just another part of their children's lives. A majority of American children play sports, learn an instrument and socialize with friends from a young age. School typically does not begin for the American child until five years, which is usually the first formal school experience. And the American student does not have to strive in a competitive academic environment until late high school and into college as the American educational system is focused on any achievement, not just high grades.

Work collaboratively in groups to produce a 5-minute video illustrating your comprehension of Chinese and American education systems.

2-2　Unit 2 译文及答案

Unit 3
Traffic and Transportation

Unit Objectives

· To acquire vocabulary and expressions related to traffic and transportation in China and the West.

· To gain a general knowledge of the characteristics of traffic and transportation in China and the West.

· To express informed opinions and thoughtful analysis about traffic and transportation.

· To develop a sense of appreciation and confidence in Chinese traffic innovation.

Read and Discuss

Read the following paragraph and discuss the following questions.

Promoting the greening and low-carbon transformation of economic and social development is a key aspect of achieving high-quality development. Accelerate the adjustment and optimization of industrial structure, energy structure, transportation structure, and more. Implement a comprehensive strategy for conservation, advance the efficient utilization of various resources, and expedite the establishment of a waste recycling system. Enhance the financial, fiscal, investment, pricing policies, and standards system that support green development. Develop green and low-carbon industries, establish a market-oriented allocation system for resource and environmental factors, accelerate the research and development as well as the widespread application of advanced energy-saving and carbon-reduction technologies. Advocate for green consumption and drive the formation of green, low-carbon production and lifestyle patterns.

1. What are the potential challenges and obstacles in implementing a comprehensive strategy for conservation and establishing a waste recycling system to promote green and low-carbon development?

2. How can governments and industries effectively incentivize the development and adoption of advanced energy-saving and carbon-reduction technologies? What role does research and development play in this process?

3. What are the social and economic benefits of advocating for green consumption and fostering green, low-carbon production and lifestyle patterns?

Section A

▼ Knowledge Focus

Ⅰ. Fill in the blanks based on your understanding of the online video lectures.

••• *Traffic Laws and Regulations in China* •••

The official driving code in China is the Law of the People's Republic of China on Road Traffic Safety. It sets strict requirements for drivers. By law, seat belts must be worn in the front and rear seats of cars where provided and it is illegal to use a hand-held mobile phone while driving. Harsh penalties are put in place for 1) _____ and driving by people

3-1
Traffic Laws and Regulations in China
扫码观看视频

who do not hold a valid driver's license or drive a vehicle without number plates. Now drunk driving is considered a criminal offence.

The penalty for 2)＿＿＿＿＿ accidents, besides criminal penalties, is 3)＿＿＿＿＿ of one's driver's license. The expressway speed limit is usually 4)＿＿＿＿＿ in China. The minimum speed limit on expressways is 60 km/h. Cases where drivers are speeding 50% 5)＿＿＿＿＿ the applicable speed limit will also result in the revocation of the driver's license.

The law also enforces a vehicle insurance system. Insurance is 6)＿＿＿＿＿ for all vehicle owners. Rates of insurance are calculated as a percentage of the value of the vehicle, but previous 7)＿＿＿＿＿ and the level of coverage may additionally be 8)＿＿＿＿＿.

Generally, we can see that Chinese people enjoy a 9)＿＿＿＿＿, comfortable, and advanced public transportation system. China's traffic laws and 10)＿＿＿＿＿ have become more and more sound and scientific.

II. Choose the best answer to each of the following questions.

1. What is the outstanding advantage of the high-speed rail train in China compared with the airplane?
    A. Affordability.
    B. Punctuality.
    C. Convenience.
    D. Seating comfort.

2. Which of the following statement about driving in China is NOT true?
    A. If foreigners are staying in China for a short period, they can apply for a temporary driving permit.
    B. The official driving code in China is the Law of the People's Republic of China on Road Traffic Safety.
    C. Those foreigners staying for shorter time have to apply for an official Chinese driver's license.
    D. The penalty for hit-and-run accidents, besides criminal penalties, is permanent revocation of one's driver's license.

3. What technology is recommended to book a taxi during rush hours in major Chinese cities?
    A. Phone call.
    B. Hand signal on the street.
    C. Taxi-hailing apps like DiDi.
    D. Sending a text message.

4. What does the Chinese law enforce regarding vehicle insurance?
   A. It's optional.
   B. It's mandatory for large vehicles only.
   C. It's mandatory for all vehicle owners.
   D. It's mandatory for vehicles older than 5 years.

5. What is the primary reason for developing new energy vehicles?
   A. To reduce fuel costs.
   B. To protect the environment.
   C. To increase vehicle speed.
   D. To enhance engine power.

6. What advantage does a plug-in hybrid vehicle have over a pure electric vehicle?
   A. Longer range.
   B. Shorter charging time.
   C. Higher speed.
   D. Lower cost.

7. What is the significance of the American brand Ford in the car industry?
   A. It is the first car brand invented in America.
   B. It represents luxury cars for presidents.
   C. It is a good representative of massive production in the car industry.
   D. It is the most expensive car brand in America.

8. What can we learn about public transportation in America?
   A. It is generally as comprehensive or efficient as in other countries.
   B. It is generally more comprehensive or efficient than that in other countries.
   C. It is generally less comprehensive or efficient than that in other countries.
   D. It has longer history and higher reputation compared with the other countries.

9. Which of the following statement about the American driving rules is NOT true?
   A. Most car rental agencies only accept international driver's license.
   B. Traffic signs and speed limits are supposed to bear in mind by all qualified drivers.
   C. Driving laws in America vary slightly from state to state.
   D. People should wear seat belts no matter they are driving or taking a car.

10. Why do American teenagers regard having their own car as a big deal?
A. Because it gives them a sense of pride.
B. Because it gives them a sense of independence.
C. Because it gives them a sense of self-dignity.
D. Because it gives them a sense of freedom.

Ⅲ. Decide whether each of the following statements is true (T) or false (F).

1. A foreigner who will stay in China for less than three months can drive in China with a foreign driving license.

2. Seat belts must be worn where provided but it is legal to use a hand-held mobile phone while driving when necessary.

3. In recent years, China's cities are gearing up for the development of hydrogen fuel cell energy, another green energy solution for vehicles.

4. A representative of the pure electric car brands—NIO, which is said to be a Tesla killer.

5. Pure electric vehicles have longer ranges compared to hybrid electric vehicles.

6. In the beginning of 2021, Tesla products in China repeatedly reported safety and quality problems.

7. American college students often get their driver's licenses at the age of eighteen.

8. The penalty for hit-and-run accidents in China is only permanent revocation of the driving license.

9. In the United States, the letter "I" in road names indicates an Interstate Highway, "Rte" signifies a local or state highway, and "U. S." represents a U. S. Highway.

10. Tesla's battery packs, which boast a set of more than 7,000 batteries, still willcatch fire when they're short-circuited.

Language Focus

I. Match the words and definitions.

____counterpart   ____dynamometer   ____marshal   ____parameter
____particulate   ____protectionist   ____retailing   ____revolutionize
____subsidiary   ____sustainable

A. connected with something but less important than it

B. relating to, or in the form of, particles

C. to gather together and organize the people, things, ideas, etc. that you need for a particular purpose

D. to completely change the way that something is done

E. a person or thing that has the same position or function as somebody/something else in a different place or situation

F. something that decides or limits the way in which something can be done

G. an advocate of government economic protection for domestic producers through restrictions on foreign competitors

H. involving the use of natural products and energy in a way that does not harm the environment

I. an instrument which measures the power output of an engine

J. the business of selling goods to the public, usually through shops/stores

II. There are 10 errors altogether in the following paragraph(s). The errors are: missing words, unnecessary words and wrong words. Please correct them as follows: for a missing word, mark its position with the symbol "∧" and write it; for an unnecessary word, cross it out with the symbol "\"; for a wrong word, underline it and write the correct word.

China now has the largest and fastest high-speed rail network in the world. It is the principle mode of long-distance transport in China. The total height of China's high-speed	1._____ 2._____

rail network reached 38,000km by 2020, included in a rail length of over 146,000km. A 2,298km Beijing-Guangzhou high-speed line is the world's longest high-speed railway line. The high-speed rail train has great reduced people's travel time. Comparing with the airplane, the outstanding advantage of the high-speed rail train is punctuality, while it is basically not effected by weather or traffic control. It has transformed the way people live and became the favorite option for business travelers today. More and more people also travel by high-speed rail train during holidays. The speed of China's high-speed rail train will continue to increase, more cities will build high-speed rail stations. With a business card of new China, high-speed rail trains are also becoming a popular choice for people in many foreign cities.

3. _____

4. _____
5. _____
6. _____
7. _____

8. _____

9. _____
10. _____

Critical Thinking

Discuss the following questions in small groups and share your ideas in class.

1. What are the current trends in transportation development in both China and the United States?

2. What are some of the reasons for the differences in the development of high-speed rail networks between China and the United States?

3. What are the potential benefits and drawbacks of widespread adoption of electric vehicles in both China and the United States?

4. Based on current trends, what might be the future of transportation development in both China and the United States?

5. How do government policies and regulations impact the development of the transportation industry in China and the United States?

6. What steps can individuals take to reduce their carbon footprint and contribute to the development of sustainable transportation systems?

Case Study

Li Wei, a Chinese exchange student, recently arrived in a mid-sized American city to attend university. One day, he decided to explore the city by taking the public bus. As he waited at the bus stop, he noticed some striking differences in traffic behavior compared to his home country. In China, when waiting for a bus, people typically form a queue in an orderly manner. Li Wei is used to standing in line, patiently waiting for his turn to board the bus. However, at the American bus stop, he observed that people didn't form a strict line but rather stood in a more dispersed manner. As the bus arrived, there was a rush of people approaching the doors all at once, without a clear order. Li Wei hesitated for a moment, unsure of the appropriate way to proceed. He decided to follow the lead of the others and joined the group near the bus doors. As he got on the bus, he noticed that there were empty seats available, but no one was sitting next to each other, leaving gaps between passengers. Li Wei also noticed that some passengers on the bus were engaged in loud phone conversations, and others were eating snacks.

Please write a summary of the scenario and analyze it from the cross-cultural perspective.

Section B

Passage 1

China's Unique Approach to Electric Vehicles

[1] If you want to overtake your competitors, you should do so when they change direction. This piece of Chinese wisdom comes from a test engineer at the National Automobile Quality

Supervision and Test Centre (NAST) in Xiangyang. He said this is the answer to a question about how likely it was that the Chinese automotive industry would play a leading role in the market for electric vehicles. Over recent years, China has put in place the most ambitious strategies of any nation in the world for getting electric cars on the roads all over the country. It is also in a good position to overtake Western nations in the race for the transport transition.

Geely subsidiary causes a surprise

[2] A tour of 2017's Shanghai Motor Show made it clear how much effort Chinese carmakers are putting into the development of electric cars. The well-known manufacturers at the motor show succeeded in attracting attention with concept cars that in some cases were highly impressive. These included the I. D. Crozz SUV coupé from Volkswagen and the technically identical Vision E concept car from Skoda. Audi presented its e-tron Sportback concept to demonstrate that it will be able to supply an electric car with a range of more than 500 km at some point. Moreover, the large numbers of Chinese manufacturers with far more electric cars on show had more definite plans. Many of their cars are already available to buy. These include models from BYD (Build Your Dreams) and also from German Chinese joint ventures such as Saic (with Volkswagen), FAW (with Audi) and Brilliance (with BMW). Ford is also planning to produce electric cars from next year onwards in cooperation with its partner Changan. However, it was the Geely subsidiary Lynk & Co that caught people's attention. Its models will be on sale in China this year and will be available in Europe in 2018, but the surprising fact was that it intends to revolutionize car retailing by selling its vehicles online. Another surprise this year was the large number of Chinese start-ups that plan to sell electric cars in large volumes.

China's unique approach to electric vehicles

[3] In the Middle Kingdom, the automotive industry is highly respected, which is one of the reasons why Internet billionaires are becoming involved in the business with the aim of repeating the Elon Musk story in China. The Chinese government's subsidy policy, which is to a certain extent protectionist, is playing into their hands and is also bringing fortune-hunters into the game. For the first time, electric cars made in China were tested to the WLTP (Worldwide Harmonized Light Vehicle Test Procedure) standard and the results surprised even the experts from Germany.

Chinese electric cars tested to the WLTP standard for the first time

[4] The NAST test center is located on a huge site and employs more than 1,000 people. These include engineers, test drivers, marshals and even gardeners who maintain the woods and green areas between the test tracks. Every car manufacturer that wants to sell its vehicles on the Chinese market must have them certified by NAST. As a result, there is always a great deal happening on the site. NAST made one of its test rigs available for the week-long assessment procedure.

[5] The cars' range and electricity consumption were measured on an AVL dynamometer on the basis of the WLTP standard for the first time in China. The Dewe2-A4 all-in-one power analyzer from Dewetron was used to measure a selection of electric parameters. The company, which is based in Graz, Austria, specializes in producing power measurement systems. In addition to using test rigs, the cars were also tested in real-life conditions on public roads. Experienced test drivers from NAST had to make their way through the traffic chaos in Xiangyang, a city with 5.84 million residents.

Surprising results from Chinese electric car manufacturers

[6] Even Truls Thorstensen, the CEO of EFS, found the results surprising. "Most of the manufacturers have succeeded in significantly improving the quality of their products. That applies not only to the materials, the paint, the finish and the look-and-feel, but also to the coordination of the powertrain and its integration into the car, which surprised me," he says. When we ask whether the vehicles meet European standards, he replies that "in this respect the Geely Borui is exactly the same as a medium-sized German car. You wouldn't notice the difference". But this was by no means the only surprise. The measurements of the electric parameters made by EFS show that Chinese electric cars could start to overtake their Western counterparts in just a few years' time. The cars' ranges in particular may well cause a sensation. Although the BYD Qin 300 with a range of 219 km according to the WLTP standard is beaten by the Tesla P85, the tiny Chinese Zhidou model from Geely with a range of 130 km leaves the BMW i3 (120 km) behind. These are measurements taken on the test rig. However, it is worth mentioning at this point that neither the Zhidou nor the BYD meet the standards required by European car buyers.

The hype is organized by the state

[7] However, the Chinese market for electric cars is growing so rapidly that even one of the most influential managers in the German automotive industry, Herbert Diess, Chairman of the Board of Management of the Volkswagen passenger cars brand, is convinced that "China will become the leading market for electromobility". For Jörg Ohlsen, CEO of Edag Engineering GmbH, alongside the state subsidies "the low local production costs are an important factor in the hype". It is not only concerns about the high particulate levels that are prompting the government in Beijing to take new and more sophisticated measures in order to promote the use of electric cars on the roads of China. Electric cars are also very much a matter of prestige. Christopher Marquis, professor in sustainable global enterprise at Cornell University in Ithaca, USA, is certain of this: "The automobile sector is something that gives a lot of prestige to countries". China sees leadership in the automotive industry as a way to raise the country's profile, he says, and its government is prepared to invest in the effort. But how great is the risk that the fast pace of development will result in quality falling by the wayside? The small

manufacturers of electric cars in particular seem to be motivated by the desire to do everything possible to obtain the subsidies.

I. Answer the following questions.

1. What does the Shanghai Motor Show demonstrate Chinese carmakers' efforts in developing electric cars?

2. Why are Internet billionaires becoming involved in China's automotive industry?

3. What was surprising about the quality of Chinese electric cars according to Truls Thorstensen?

4. According to Jörg Ohlsen, what is an important factor in China's hype for electric cars?

5. Why does the government in Beijing promote the use of electric cars?

II. Translate the following paragraph into English.

青藏铁路是世界上最高最长的高原铁路,全长 1956 公里,其中有 960 公里在海拔 4000 多米之上,是连接西藏和中国其他地区的第一条铁路。由于铁路穿越世界上最脆弱的生态系统,在建设期间和建成后都采取了生态保护措施,以确保其成为一条"绿色铁路"。青藏铁路大大缩短了中国内地与西藏之间的旅行时间。更重要的是,它极大地促进了西藏的经济发展,改善了当地居民的生活。铁路开通后,愈来愈多的人选择乘火车前往西藏,这样还有机会欣赏沿线的美景。

▼ Passage 2

✧✦✧ *The Price of Oil and the Price of Carbon* ✧✦✧

[A] Fossil fuel prices are likely to stay "low for long". Notwithstanding important recent progress in developing renewable fuel sources, low fossil fuel prices could discourage further innovation in, and adoption of, cleaner energy technologies. The result would be higher emissions of carbon dioxide and other greenhouse gases.

[B] Policymakers should not allow low energy prices to derail the clean energy transition. Action to restore appropriate price incentives, notably through corrective carbon pricing, is urgently needed to lower the risk of irreversible and potentially devastating effects of climate change. That approach also offers fiscal benefits.

[C] Oil prices have dropped by over 60% since June 2014. A commonly held view in the oil industry is that "the best cure for low oil prices is low oil prices". The reasoning behind this saying is that low oil prices discourage investment in new production capacity, eventually shifting the oil supply curve backward and bringing prices back up as existing oil fields— which can be tapped at relatively low marginal cost— are depleted. In fact, in line with past experience capital expenditure in the oil sector has dropped sharply in many producing countries, including the United States. The dynamic adjustment to low oil prices may, however, be different this time around.

[D] Oil prices are expected to remain lower for longer. The advent of new technologies has added about 4.2 million barrels per day to the crude oil market, contributing to a global over-supply. In addition, other factors are putting downward pressure on oil prices: change in the strategies behavior of the Organization of Petroleum Exporting Countries, the projected increase in Iranian exports, the scaling-down of global demand (especially from emerging markets), the long-term drop in petroleum consumption in the United States, and some displacement of oil by substitutes. These likely persistent forces, like the growth of shale (页岩) oil, point to a "low for long" scenario. Futures markets, which show only a modest recovery of prices to around $60 a barrel by 2019, support this view.

[E] Natural gas and coal— also fossil fuels— have similarly seen price declines that look to be long-lived. Coal and natural gas are mainly used for electricity generation, whereas oil is used mostly to power transportation, yet the prices of all these energy sources are linked. The North American shale gas boom has resulted in record low prices there. The recent discovery of the giant Zohr gas field off the Egyptian coast will eventually have impact on pricing in the Mediterranean region and Europe, and there is significant development potential in many other places, notably Argentina. Coal prices also are low, owing to over-supply and the scaling-down of demand, especially from China, which bums half of the world's coal.

[F] Technological innovations have unleashed the power of renewables such as wind, hydro, solar, and geothermal (地热). Even Africa and the Middle East, home to economies that are heavily dependent on fossil fuel exports, have enormous potential to develop renewables. For example, the United Arab Emirates has endorsed an ambitious target to draw 24% of its primary energy consumption from renewable sources by 2021.

[G] Progress in the development of renewables could be fragile, however, if fossil fuel prices remain low for long. Renewables account for only a small share of global primary energy consumption, which is still dominated by fossil fuels— 30% each for coal and oil, 25% for natural gas. But renewable energy will have to displace fossil fuels to a much greater extent in the future to avoid unacceptable climate risks.

[H] Unfortunately, the current low prices for oil, gas, and coal may provide little incentive for research to find even cheaper substitutes for those fuels. There is strong evidence that both innovation and adoption of cleaner technology are strongly encouraged by higher fossil fuel prices. The same is true for new technologies for alleviating fossil fuel emissions.

[I] The current low fossil fuel price environment will thus certainly delay the energy transition from fossil fuel to clean energy sources. Unless renewables become cheap enough that substantial carbon deposits are left underground for a very long time, if not forever, the planet will like be exposed to potentially catastrophic climate risks.

[J] Some climate impacts may already be discernible. For example, the United Nations Children Fund estimates that some 11 million children in Africa face hunger, disease, and water shortage as a result of the strongest El Nino (厄尔尼诺) weather phenomenon in decades. Many scientists believe that El Nino events, caused by warming in the Pacific, are becoming more intense as a result of climate change.

[K] Nations from around the world have gathered in Paris for the United Nations Climate Change Conference, COP 21, with the goal of a universal and potentially legally-binding agreement reducing greenhouse gas emissions. We need very broad participation to fully address global tragedy that results when countries fail to take into account the negative impact of their carbon emissions on the rest of the world. Moreover, non-participation by nations, if sufficiently widespread, can undermine the political will of participating countries to act.

[L] The nations participating at COP 21 are focusing on quantitative emissions-reduction commitments. Economic reasoning shows that the least expensive way for each country is to put a price on carbon emissions. The reason is that when carbon is priced, those emissions reductions that are least costly to implement will happen first. The International Monetary Fund calculates that countries can generate substantial fiscal revenues by eliminating fossil fuel subsidies and levying carbon charges that capture the domestic damage caused by emissions. A tax on upstream carbon sources is one easy way to put a price on carbon emissions, although some countries may wish to use other methods, such as emissions trading schemes. In order to maximize global welfare, every country's carbon pricing should reflect not only the purely domestic damage from emissions, but also the damage to foreign countries.

[M] Setting the right carbon price will therefore efficiently align the costs paid by carbon users with the true social opportunity cost of using carbon. By raising relative demand for clean energy sources, a carbon price would also help align the market return to clean-energy innovation with its social return, spurring the refinement of existing technologies and the development of new ones. And it would raise the demand for technologies such as carbon capture and storage, spurring their further development. If not corrected by the appropriate carbon price, low fossil fuel prices are not accurately signaling to markets the true social profitability of clean energy. While alternative estimates of the damage from carbon emissions differ, and it's especially hard to reckon the likely costs of possible catastrophic climate events, most estimates suggest substantial negative effects.

[N] Direct subsidies to research and development have been adopted by some governments but are a poor substitute for a carbon price; they do only part of the job, leaving in place market incentives to overuse fossil fuels and thereby add to the stock of atmospheric greenhouse gases without regard to the collateral (附带的) costs.

[O] The hope is that the success of COP 21 opens the door to future international agreement on carbon prices. Agreement on an international carbon-price floor would be a good starting point in that process. Failure to address comprehensively the problem of greenhouse gas emissions, however, exposes all generations, present and future, to incalculable risks.

Ⅰ. **Fast reading.**

Direction: Each statement of the following contains information given in one of the paragraphs in the above passage. Identify the paragraph from which the information is derived. You may choose a paragraph more than once. Each paragraph is marked with a letter.

1. A number of factors are driving down the global oil prices not just for now but in the foreseeable future.

2. Pricing carbon proves the most economical way to reduce greenhouse gas emissions.

3. It is estimated that extreme weather conditions have endangered the lives of millions of African children.

4. The prices of coal are low as a result of over-supply and decreasing demand.

5. Higher fossil fuel prices prove to be conducive to innovation and application of cleaner technology.

6. If fossil fuel prices remain low for a long time, it may lead to higher emissions of greenhouse gases.

7. Fossil fuels remain the major source of primary energy consumption in today's world.

8. Even major fossil fuel exporting countries have great potential to develop renewable energies.

9. Greenhouse gas emissions, if not properly dealt with, will pose endless risks for mankind.

10. It is urgent for governments to increase the cost of using fossil fuels to an appropriate level to lessen the catastrophic effects of climate change.

II. **Translate the following paragraph into Chinese.**

American traffic and transportation systems vary widely across regions due to the country's vastness and diverse urban planning. While cities like New York and San Francisco have well-developed public transit networks, many areas rely heavily on personal vehicles. Highways and roads form the backbone of American transportation, reflecting the nation's car-centric culture. The expansive road infrastructure can lead to traffic congestion, particularly in major urban centers. Additionally, ride-sharing services and the gradual adoption of electric vehicles are influencing the transportation landscape. The diversity in transportation preferences and infrastructure highlights the complexity of catering to both urban and rural mobility needs in the United States.

Cross-cultural Perspectives

Read the following paragraph and write a summary of 200 words.

●●● *Cultural Difference between Chinese and American* ●●●

Traffic and Transportation Systems

[1] Traffic and transportation are integral components of any modern society, serving as the lifeblood of economic and social activities. China and the United States, two of the world's largest and most influential nations, possess vastly different traffic and transportation systems. These differences arise from historical, cultural, and geographical factors, shaping not only the daily lives of their citizens but also impacting their economies and environmental sustainability. In this article, we will delve into the distinctions between Chinese and American traffic and transportation systems, exploring their infrastructure, modes of transport, regulatory frameworks, and the broader implications of these differences.

Infrastructure and urban planning

[2] One of the most striking differences between Chinese and American transportation systems is the sheer scale and population density. Chinese cities, particularly mega-cities like

Beijing, Shanghai, and Guangzhou, have developed extensive public transportation networks and invested heavily in high-speed railways and modern highways to cater to their large populations. In contrast, many American cities have a lower population density and are more car-centric, relying heavily on private automobiles.

[3] China is a world leader in high-speed rail, with an extensive network that spans thousands of miles, connecting major cities. This network is known for its speed, efficiency, and affordability. In contrast, the United States has lagged in high-speed rail development, with only limited projects like Amtrak's Acela Express and the California High-Speed Rail in progress.

[4] Chinese cities boast extensive public transportation systems, including subways, buses, trams, and bike-sharing programs. These systems are often heavily subsidized, making them affordable and accessible to a wide range of citizens. In the United States, public transportation varies widely from city to city, with some major cities offering comprehensive systems (e.g., New York City's subway) while others have limited options.

Modes of transport

[5] The United States is known for its love affair with the automobile. American cities are designed around the car, and a majority of citizens rely on private vehicles for their daily commute. The result is congested highways and high levels of air pollution in many urban areas. In contrast, Chinese cities have implemented policies to limit the number of private vehicles on the road, using measures such as license plate lotteries and congestion pricing to combat traffic congestion and reduce emissions.

[6] China has experienced a resurgence of bicycles and electric scooters as a sustainable mode of transportation. Companies like Ofo and Mobike introduced bike-sharing programs that quickly gained popularity in Chinese cities. In the United States, while bike-sharing and electric scooter rental services exist, they are less widespread and face regulatory challenges in many cities.

[7] Both China and the United States have embraced ridesharing and e-hailing services like Uber and Didi Chuxing. However, these services have faced regulatory challenges in both countries, with local governments seeking to balance innovation with safety and competition.

Regulatory framework

[8] The transportation sector in China is heavily influenced by government control and investment. State-owned enterprises play a significant role in developing and operating transportation infrastructure. In contrast, the United States relies more on private sector involvement, with companies like Ford, GM, and Tesla driving innovation in the automotive industry.

[9] Environmental sustainability is a growing concern in both countries, but their approaches differ. China has been investing in electric buses and vehicles to combat air pollution, with the government setting ambitious goals for the adoption of electric vehicles (EVs). The United States has a more decentralized approach, with individual states and cities setting their own policies and incentives for EV adoption.

Implications and future trends

[10] Transportation systems have a profound impact on the economies of both countries. In China, the extensive high-speed rail network has facilitated the movement of goods and people, supporting economic growth. In the United States, a heavy reliance on private automobiles can lead to congestion, productivity losses, and increased infrastructure maintenance costs.

[11] Both countries are grappling with environmental challenges caused by transportation. China's push for electric vehicles and public transportation aims to reduce air pollution and combat climate change. In the United States, there is a growing awareness of the need to reduce greenhouse gas emissions from the transportation sector, but progress varies by state.

[12] Both China and the United States are investing in cutting-edge transportation technologies. China is a leader in electric and autonomous vehicles, while the United States has a strong presence in electric and self-driving car development. The competition in this space will likely drive innovation and shape the future of transportation.

[13] Chinese and American traffic and transportation systems reflect the unique characteristics and priorities of each nation. China's emphasis on extensive public transportation networks, high-speed rail, and government-led initiatives has allowed it to address the challenges of rapid urbanization and population growth. In contrast, the United States' reliance on private vehicles and a decentralized approach to transportation planning presents its own set of challenges, including traffic congestion and environmental concerns.

[14] As both countries continue to evolve their transportation systems to meet the needs of their citizens and address global challenges like climate change, there is much that they can learn from each other. Collaborative efforts and knowledge sharing could lead to more efficient,

sustainable, and innovative transportation systems that benefit not only China and the United States but also the world as a whole.

Case Study

The transportation systems of China and the USA provide a compelling insight into how cultural differences influence urban mobility strategies. These countries, with their distinct societal values and historical contexts, manifest unique approaches to traffic management, public transportation, and personal mobility.

In China, rapid urbanization and a collective mindset have driven the development of extensive public transportation systems. Cities like Beijing and Shanghai have invested heavily in metro networks, reflecting a cultural emphasis on shared resources and efficient utilization of space. The high adoption rate of bikes and e-scooters echoes China's historical affinity for bicycles and its drive for sustainable mobility. Additionally, Chinese cities are experimenting with innovative solutions like bike-sharing programs, showcasing a willingness to adapt to contemporary challenges.

On the other hand, the US's car-centric culture has shaped urban landscapes to accommodate personal vehicles. Wide roads, extensive parking lots, and the iconic American highway system reflect a cultural attachment to individual autonomy and convenience. This approach, however, has led to issues like traffic congestion and air pollution. Despite this, American cities such as New York and San Francisco emphasize public transit and pedestrian-friendly areas, reflecting a growing cultural shift towards sustainable mobility practices.

Cultural norms also affect pedestrian behavior and road safety. In China, the fluid movement of pedestrians, bikes, and cars within shared spaces signifies a culture of adaptability and cooperation. Crossing the street in bustling Chinese cities requires a blend of assertiveness and flexibility. In contrast, American streets are often more structured, with pedestrians adhering to crosswalks and traffic signals, reflecting a culture of lawfulness and individual rights.

Cultural attitudes towards privacy and personal space also influence transportation preferences. In China, ride-sharing services like Didi Chuxing are popular, as people are accustomed to sharing rides with strangers due to densely populated urban areas. In the USA, ride-sharing services like Uber and Lyft faced initial resistance due to concerns over personal privacy and security, highlighting the cultural value placed on individual boundaries.

Both countries showcase different modes of transportation due to these cultural influences. China's commitment to shared mobility aligns with its collective ethos, while the USA's infrastructure investments cater to a culture of individualism and personal convenience. Understanding these cultural nuances is vital for crafting transportation policies that align with societal values, enabling more sustainable, efficient, and culturally sensitive urban mobility solutions.

Work collaboratively in groups to produce a 5-minute video illustrating your comprehension of the traffic and transportation that exemplify the cultural disparities between China and the United States.

3-2　Unit 3 译文及答案

Unit 4
Festivals and Celebrations

Unit Objectives

· To acquire vocabulary and expressions related to festivals and celebrations in China and the West.

· To gain a general knowledge of the characteristics of festivals and celebrations in China and the West.

· To express informed opinions and thoughtful analysis about festivals.

· To develop a sense of appreciation and confidence in Chinese festivals.

Read and Discuss

Read the following paragraph and discuss the following questions.

During the Spring Festival, when members of a family get together, we feel that reunion is happiness and unity is strength. Family has always been valued by the Chinese people and harmony in a family makes everything successful. We should nurture and practice core socialist values, foster the traditional virtues of the Chinese nation, and love both family and the country. We should pool the wisdom and strength of more than 1.3 billion Chinese people in more than 400 million households to strive for the great success of socialism with Chinese characteristics for a new era and realize the Chinese Dream of national rejuvenation.

1. Apart from family reunions, what are some other ways in which Chinese people express their value for family?
_____

2. What does "the Chinese Dream of national rejuvenation" mean?
_____

3. Why is the Spring Festival considered an important occasion for family reunions in Chinese culture?
_____

Section A

▼ Knowledge Focus

Ⅰ. Fill in the blanks based on your understanding of the online video lectures.

●●● *Spring Festival* ●●●

In Chinese spoken language, celebrating Chinese spring festival is pronounced as "guo nian", because the origin of spring festival is related with a 1)_____ called Nian. Nian was said to be a monster beast that 2)_____ on human being at the night before the beginning of a new year and it caused 3)_____ to the towns and village every year. One day, an old man came to their rescue, offering to 4)_____ "Nian". He found that the monster was afraid of loud noise and people in red clothes, so he defeated it by 5)_____ to make lots of noises. Later on, people put up red paper decorations on windows and doors, and play fireworks at the end of each year to scare away "Nian" in case it 6)_____ back again. Thus, the celebration was called "guo nian", which means 7)_____ the monster Nian in Chinese.

4-1
Spring Festival
扫码观看视频

As time goes by, folk tales, which spread from generation to generation orally, change a lot. There is another 8) _____ of the story in which the monster is called Xi. The other parts of the story were similar to that of Nian. It was 9) _____ by red clothes and noisy firecrackers. So, another name of the Chinese New Year eve is "ChuXi", which means 10) _____ the monster Xi.

Ⅱ. Choose the best answer to each of the following questions.

1. What is one of the typical preparations people make before the New Year's Eve during the Spring Festival?

   A. Planting new trees.

   B. Moving to the new house.

   C. Learning a new language.

   D. Buying some new clothes.

2. When is the official end of the Spring Festival?

   A. January 31st.

   B. February 1st.

   C. Lantern festival.

   D. February 15th.

3. What is the significance of putting up red decorations on doors during the Spring Festival?

   A. It symbolizes protection against evil spirits.

   B. It represents good luck and prosperity for the household.

   C. It indicates the arrival of spring and new beginnings.

   D. It marks the end of the winter season.

4. During the Spring Festival, what kind of words should be avoided to maintain a positive atmosphere?

   A. Words related to bad weather and natural disasters.

   B. Words with negative connotations such as defeat, illness, or death.

   C. Words associated with work-related stress and challenges.

   D. Words expressing personal grievances and complaints.

5. Why was May 20, 2015, a significant date for the Qixi Festival?

   A. It marked the publication of a famous love story.

   B. It was the date of an important astronomical event.

   C. The Qixi Festival was officially recognized as Intangible Cultural Heritage.

   D. It was the anniversary of Niulang and Zhinv's reunion.

6. Which one of the following statements about the first European settlers is NOT true?

A. They are religious separatists seeking a new home to freely practice their faith.

B. They are individuals lured by the promise of prosperity and land ownership in the New World.

C. They sailed across the Atlantic Ocean to settle in the New World.

D. They taught the Native tribe how to grow corn and how to hunt and fish.

7. What can we learn about the typical traditional dishes of the Thanksgiving dinner?

A. Turkey will be mainly cooked in such way as smoked.

B. Pumpkin pie is made from the fresh and sweet pumpkin of the summer.

C. Corn represents the harvest and the fall season.

D. Cranberry sauce is made from native American fruit.

8. Which activity in Thanksgiving celebrations will attract lots of people at the scene or in front of their TV set?

A. The Thanksgiving dinner.

B. The Thanksgiving parade.

C. Macy's promotion activity.

D. The volunteer activity.

9. Who asked all Americans to set aside the last Thursday in November as a day of thanksgiving?

A. George Washington.

B. Abraham Lincoln.

C. Andrew Jackson.

D. Thomas Jefferson.

10. Which of the following statements about the Valentine's Day is true?

A. It was commonly believed by Americans that February 14 was the beginning of bird's mating season.

B. The Valentine's Day for Americans started from a pleasant love story.

C. In America, best friends, grandparents and parents, teachers, favorite colleagues from the office, and even pets may also get a greeting on the Valentine's Day.

D. The American poet Geofftrey Chaucer was the first to record St. Valentine's Day.

Ⅲ. Decide whether each of the following statements is true (T) or false (F).

1. A coin or a sweet date is usually hidden in one of the traditional dishes served during the Spring Festival dinner.

2. Paper cuttings are usually pasted on windows as decorations during the Spring Festival and often include patterns of animals from the Chinese zodiac.

3. The Qixi Festival is celebrated in February according to the lunar calendar.

4. In the evening of Qixi, young women, sitting around the table, would play games and read poems until midnight.

5. Showing skills in cooking was the most popular custom for women in the evening of Qixi.

6. The Thanksgiving Day is often compared with the Mid-Autumn Day in Chinese culture because both are celebrations of family reunion and autumn harvest.

7. Black Friday got its name because it was originally associated with a financial crisis in the 1930s.

8. Thanksgiving Day is celebrated on the third Thursday of November.

9. Sending greeting cards on Valentine's Day was popularized in America due to mass printing of poetic Valentine's cards.

10. American school children do not participate in the tradition of exchanging Valentine's Day cards with classmates, teachers, and parents.

Language Focus

Ⅰ. Match the words and definitions.

____ bypass   ____ coincidence   ____ colonist   ____ commemorate
____ connotation ____ elaborate   ____ feast   ____ galaxy
                 ____ prey   ____ subdue

A. any of the large systems of stars, etc. in outer space

B. to remind people of an important person or event from the past with a special action or object

C. go around or avoid a place

D. to hunt and kill another animal for food

E. an idea suggested by a word in addition to its main meaning

F. the fact of two things happening at the same time by chance, in a surprising way

G. a large or special meal, especially for a lot of people and to celebrate something

H. a person who settles in an area that has become a colony

I. very complicated and detailed; carefully prepared and organized

J. to bring somebody/something under control, especially by using force

II. There are 10 errors altogether in the following paragraph(s). The errors are: missing words, unnecessary words and wrong words. Please correct them as follows: for a missing word, mark its position with the symbol "∧" and write it; for an unnecessary word, cross it out with the symbol "\"; for a wrong word, underline it and write the correct word.

How do people celebrate Valentine's Day? The traditional activity is sending greet cards to lovers. By the middle of the 18th, it was common of friends and lovers of all social classes to exchange small token of affection or handwritten notes. And by the 1900, the tradition of sending Valentines greeting becomes popular due to the Americans and their mass printing of poetic Valentine's cards. Printing cards began to replace written letters due improvements in printing technology. Ready-made cards were an easy way for people to express their emotions in a time when indirect expression of one's feelings were discouraged. Cheaper postage rates also contributed to an increase in the popular of sending Valentine's Day greetings. In the 1840s, Esther A. Howland began selling a

1. _____

2. _____

3. _____

4. _____

5. _____

6. _____

7. _____

8. _____

9. _____

first mass-produced valentines in America. Howland, known as the "Mother of the Valentine," who made elaborate creations with real lace, ribbons and colorful pictures known as "scrap".	10. _____

▼ Critical Thinking

Discuss the following questions in small groups and share your ideas in class.

1. What is the significance of the Qixi festival in Chinese culture?

2. What cultural connotations are reflected in Chinese and American traditional festivals?

3. What roles do both Chinese and Western festivals play in the modern society?

4. What can we infer about the cultural values of China and the United States from their significant holiday traditions?

5. Why are traditional festivals still inherited from generations to generations?

6. How to carry forward and further develop the spirit of traditional festivals?

▼ Case Study

15-year-old Kate invited Paul, an American exchange student from her class, to celebrate the Chinese Spring Festival in her hometown. On the second day of the lunar calendar, Kate went to visit her relatives, accompanied by Paul. As they were walking along the street, they came across a dragon dance performance. Kate started explaining the significance of the dance to Paul, but she noticed that he suddenly became very scared, with no smile on his face. Kate was puzzled and didn't understand why Paul had such a reaction.

Suppose you are Kate's sister, a college student majoring in English, please write a letter to tell Kate why Paul was scared.

Section B

◯ Passage 1

●●● A Guide to Traditional Chinese Festivals ●●●

[1] All of my life, I've marveled at the diversity and number of Chinese celebrations and festivals. Although from a Chinese background, I'm embarrassed to say, I still struggle to remember which one is which! Each tradition has its roots and origins, some dating back all the way to the beginnings of Chinese civilization. Here are some of the most famous festivals and celebrations of the Chinese tradition

Chinese New Year

[2] The Chinese New Year is a 15-day celebration that marks the beginning of the lunar calendar year. As such, this holiday is also called the Lunar New Year or the Spring Festival. According to legend, this celebration began over 3000 years ago during the Shang Dynasty (1600 BC-1046 BC).

[3] Back then, a beast named Nian (年) or "Year" was said to come out on Lunar New Year's Eve to harm people, destroy their property, and generally serve as a major nuisance. Eventually, the people discovered that Nian feared the color red, loud sounds, and fire. This is the reason why red and loud firecrackers are so prevalent during this holiday.

[4] Nowadays, with the beast Nian taken care of, the entire family gathers together for a feast of epic proportions. Festivities include fireworks, dragon dances, spending quality time with family and friends, feasting on scrumptious Chinese treats, the giving of red envelopes filled with cash (hongbao), and decorating windows and doors with red paper-cut couplets.

[5] Also on this day, families get together to make and enjoy dumplings. Most people today associate dumplings with wealth and fortune, since they resemble the shape of ancient silver and gold ingots.

[6] However, another origin story for dumplings says they were born out of the kindness of an ancient Chinese doctor who healed an entire village with his special ear-shaped dumpling recipe.

The Moon Festival

[7] This is the greatest holiday of the Chinese autumn, when the moon is biggest and

roundest, and families gather together. Just replace the turkey with some mooncakes, light up some lanterns and fireworks, and enjoy time with family. Moon-watching is a must if the skies are clear.

[8] There are several stories associated with this festival. One is the legend of the Chinese moon goddess Chang'e. To make a long story short, her husband found some immortality elixir, Chang'e grew impatient and drank the entire bottle, and ended up flying to the moon (with only a jade rabbit to keep her company).

[9] Another story claims that the festival was inspired by an uprising against the Mongol rulers of the Yuan Dynasty (1271-1368). During that time, group gatherings were banned to prevent potential uprisings. However, one rebel advisor, Liu Bowen, noticed that Mongols never ate mooncakes. He devised a plan to get permission to distribute thousands of mooncakes to Chinese residents in the city on the night of the Moon festival, ostentatiously to celebrate the emperor's longevity.

[10] In reality, each mooncake was embedded with a message that said: "Kill the Mongols on the 15th day of the 8th lunar month!" Thus, a coordinated attack overthrew the government that night and established the Ming Dynasty (1368-1644) under rebel leader Zhu Yuanzhang. Mooncakes attained national snack-food status for the festival ever afterwards.

Lantern Festival

[11] The Lantern Festival marks the end of Chinese New Year celebrations, on the fifteenth day of the new lunar year. On this day, families gather to eat food, decorate lanterns, and then release their mini hot-air balloons into the sky.

[12] The origin of this festival dates back to the Han Dynasty (202 BC-220) when Buddhist monks would hang lanterns on the 15th day of the lunar year in honor of the Buddha. This custom was observed by the general population and later spread throughout China and East Asia.

[13] The more recent addition of the sky-floating lanterns is said to have come from the brilliant tactician Zhuge Liang (181-234), who first used one of these floating lights to signal for reinforcements during a battle when his army was surrounded. Today, however, these lanterns are more of a symbol of the harmony between our world and the divine as they float ever closer to the heavens.

[14] A special snack to eat during this festival would be the small glutinous rice balls called tangyuan. Shaped into perfect little spheres of joy and then boiled, these tasty treats are filled with fruit, nuts, or sesame, and symbolize wholeness and family unity.

Dragon Boat Festival

[15] Occurring on the 5th day of the 5th month of the lunar calendar, the Dragon Boat Festival is one of the most upbeat and fun festivals in Chinese culture. Its origins, however, come from a story of tragic heroism.

[16] Back during the Warring States period (475 BC-221 BC) of the Zhou Dynasty, an upright official named Qu Yuan lived in the state of Chu. When the King of Chu made an alliance with the powerful state of Qin, Qu Yuan was banished and accused of treason because he severely opposed the alliance. After 28 years, Qin broke the alliance and invaded Chu, prompting Qu Yuan to drown himself in despair in the Miluo River.

[17] The local villagers admired him deeply and raced out in boats to save him or at least retrieve his body. This is said to be the origin of the dragon boat race. When the villagers couldn't find his body, they threw balls of sticky rice into the river so the fish could eat them instead of eating Qu Yuan's body.

[18] Today, these delicious balls of sticky rice, known as zongzi, are an essential part of any Dragon Boat celebration. This tasty Chinese dish is made with balls of rice stuffed with different fillings then wrapped in bamboo leaves.

Qingming Festival

[19] The Qingming Festival, also known as Tomb-Sweeping Day in English, is celebrated on the 15th day after the Spring Equinox (either April 4th or 5th of a given year).

[20] The origin of this festival dates back to China's Spring and Autumn period around 650 BC. A prince named Wen was exiled in his childhood to avoid religious persecution. He had a loyal attendant by the name of Jie Zitui who was always by his side.

[21] Nineteen years later, Prince Wen successfully returned home and succeeded the throne. He rewarded his many attendants who remained by his side, with one exception: his most loyal attendant Jie Zitui. Jie Zitui chose to silently live in a remote mountain and not ask for any rewards. When Emperor Wen finally felt guilty for his actions, he went to the mountain to find Jie Zitui. When Jie refused to see him, Emperor Wen set fire to the mountain to coax him into coming down.

[22] Jie, however, still did not come down and he hugged a willow tree until his death. Emperor Wen felt so full of regret that he decided in order to commemorate his former loyal attendant, he would set this day as the Hanshi Festival which is now known today as the Qingming Festival. On this day, families would get together and pay respects to their ancestors.

Double Ninth Festival

[23] This festival has two other names: The Chongyang Festival and the Senior Citizens' Festival. This holiday is a tradition for maintaining good health and vibrancy, while also taking the time to visit the great outdoors in the crisp fall weather.

[24] Various sources trace this holiday to the story of Huan Jing, a man who believed a pestilence was coming on the 9th day of the 9th lunar month.

[25] The book *I Ching* considered the number "nine" to be a yang number in the theory of yin and yang, and the 9th day of the 9th lunar month was a potentially dangerous date because of excess yang energy.

[26] To avoid disaster, he told his family members to climb a hill with zhuyu (dogwood) sprigs and drink chrysanthemum wine.

[27] Dogwood (Cornus officinal is to be exact), with its strong fragrance, was said to drive away evil spirits; chrysanthemum blossoms promoted longevity. Both plants were said to have cleansing qualities and the ability to cure illnesses.

[28] The family obeyed and did not return to the village until evening, when they found all their livestock dead. Huan Jing found out from his teacher, a cultivating Taoist, that the animals had died in place of his family.

[29] Following in the footsteps of Huan Jing, on this day people drink chrysanthemum tea and search for the nearest mountain to climb. If there's no mountain nearby, you can always eat some Chongyang cakes instead, since the Chinese character for cake, gao, is a homophone for height.

I. Answer the following questions.

1. Why are dumplings an important part of the Chinese New Year celebration, and what do they symbolize?

2. What are the legends associated with the Moon Festival, and how have these stories contributed to its traditions?

3. Who is Zhuge Liang, and how did he contribute to the Lantern Festival?

4. When does the Dragon Boat Festival occur in the lunar calendar, and what is its historical significance?

5. What is the significance of climbing a hill with zhuyu sprigs and drinking chrysanthemum wine during the Double Ninth Festival?

II. Translate the following paragraph into English.

贴春联(Spring Festival couplets)是中国人欢度春节的一个重要习俗。春联由一对诗句和四字横批(horizontal scroll)组成,诗句和横批用金色或黑色写在红纸上,红色代表幸运,金色代表财富。春联贴在大门左右两侧和门框上方。春联的诗句体现中国传统诗词的特点,两句诗的字数相同、内容相关。横批凸显春联的主题,更是锦上添花。春联以简洁的文字描绘生动的形象,抒发美好的愿望,当家家户户贴春联时,人们就会意识到春节已经正式拉开序幕。

Passage 2

April Fools' Day: What Are Its Origins and How Do Europeans Celebrate?

[A] While it may not be a national holiday, April Fools' Day— also called All Fools' Day—is celebrated by many countries every year on 1 April. Known for giving people a free pass to prank their partners, friends, families, colleagues and pretty much everyone, the day is seen as an opportunity to dupe the most gullible into believing the most outlandish things. The day consists of practical jokes, pranks and hoaxes. Pranksters often yell "April Fools!" at their victim, and this custom has been observed for hundreds of years.

[B] Many trace the custom back to medieval France where 25 March used to be New Year's Day until the Julian calendar was reformed in 1564 and changed to the Gregorian calendar. Before then, New Year festivities culminated on 1st April. After 1st January was officially adopted as New Year's Day, those who forgot to change the date and continued to celebrate on 1st April were ridiculed and labeled April Fools.

How is April Fools' Day celebrated in Europe?

[C] Different countries have their own unique ways of pranking their April Fools victims. In France, Belgium, Italy and French-speaking areas of Switzerland, the celebrations include sticking a paper fish onto the backs of as many people as possible without being noticed, and then yelling "Poisson d'Avril" / "Pesce d'Aprile" ("April fish!"). Many suggest that the fish might refer to young animals which are easily caught.

[D] April Fools' Day is only celebrated for half a day in England. Pranks and jokes are only permitted until noon, the etiquette states that when the clock strikes noon, you are meant to come clean about your pranks. Anyone playing a joke after midday is considered the official April fool. Handy for parents try to keep their kids in check, but come on— loosen up, lads. Significantly more fun is April Fools' Day festivities in Scotland, which last two days. It is called Gowkie Day, for the gowk— or cuckoo— a symbol of the fool.

[E] In Ireland, meanwhile, tradition dictates sending someone on a "fool's errand". The victim is sent to deliver a letter, supposedly asking for help. When the person receives the letter, they open it, read it and tell the messenger that they will have to take the letter to another person. This goes on for a while until someone feels sorry for them and shows them what the letter says: "Send the fool to someone else."

[F] In the Netherlands, citizens tend to catapult or slingshot herring in the direction of their neighbours and yell "haringgek" ("herring fool"). Germans play a prank called an "Aprilscherz" which is all about telling one outrageous but generally harmless story that's completely made up to fool others. In Greece, successfully tricking someone on this day is said to bring the prankster good luck for the entire year. The Polish handily have a warning, "Prima Aprilis— uważaj, bo się pomylisz", which translates to "April Fools' Day, be careful — you can be wrong!"

[G] Spain and Portugal both celebrate on different days. The Portuguese don't celebrate April Fools' Day on 1st April and prefer the Sunday and Monday prior to LENT. On this day, people throw flour onto unsuspecting passers-by. As for the Spanish, the day of pranks is celebrated on 28th December as Holy Innocents' Day, during which no one can be held accountable for their actions, as the pranksters are considered innocent.

April Fools' Day pranks

[H] In modern times, news outlets have participated in the 1st April tradition by going to great lengths to create elaborate hoaxes. They report a least one outrageous fictional claim published amidst other articles in order to fool their audiences. The Brits tend to do very well here. In England, it had become a popular prank to send gullible victims to the Tower of London to see the washing of the lions— a ceremony that didn't exist. The prank first appeared in a British newspaper on 2nd April 1698, where an article on the front page read: "Yesterday being the first of April, several persons were sent to the Tower Ditch to see the Lions washed." Examples of this particular hoax continued at least through the mid-1800s.

[I] Much later on, the BBC infamously reported on 1st April 1957 in a spoof segment that Swiss farmers were experiencing a record spaghetti crop and showed footage of people harvesting noodles from trees. It even had footage of women picking strands off a tree and laying them in the sun to dry. Many people were fooled, and the story had so many inquiries that they had to own up to the stunt the next day. The BBC has a decent track record in the matter. In 2008, they fooled their audience again with their viral Miracles of Evolution trailer, which appeared to show some special penguins that had regained the ability to fly.

[J] The US is also excellent when it comes to these fake stories. In 1992, National Public Radio ran a spot with former President Richard Nixon saying he was running for president again. This caught the public by surprise, and huge sighs of relief came once it was revealed that it was only an actor and not Nixon.

[K] There was also NPR's 2014 prank, in which the media outlet promoted a story on Facebook headlined: "Why Doesn't America Read Anymore?" The story sparked outrage in the post's comments section. But had the commenters actually read the article, they would have seen all it said was: "Congratulations, genuine readers, and happy April Fools' Day!"

[L] Major companies even get in on it, with Virgin Atlantic revealing the "Dreambird 1417" in 2017, which boasted wings that bend and flex to create a flapping motion that "not only propels the aircraft forward but generates its own power to meet every electronic need on board".

[M] So watch out for the information you're fed on 1 April. For example, the bit earlier about the catapulted herring in the Netherlands is utter nonsense. In the era of "fake news", it's tricky on a normal day to work out when we're being tricked into believing something that isn't true. But do make sure not to fall for absolutely everything you read or hear on April Fool's Day.

I. **Fast reading.**

Direction: Each statement of the following contains information given in one of the paragraphs in the above passage. Identify the paragraph from which the information is derived. You may choose a paragraph more than once. Each paragraph is marked with a letter.

1. Prominent corporations also participate in April Fools' Day pranks.

2. When the transition of New Year celebrations to January 1st occurred, those who mistakenly stuck to April 1st as New Year's Day were mocked and called April Fools.

3. On Holy Innocents' Day, pranksters are considered innocent, and no one is held responsible for their actions.

4. NPR surprised the public by airing a segment featuring an actor pretending to be former President Richard Nixon, announcing his candidacy for president once more.

5. According to tradition, pranks and jokes are allowed until midday, after which it's customary to confess and reveal the prank.

6. A popular English prank involved tricking unsuspecting individuals into visiting the Tower of London to witness the non-existent "washing of the lions."

7. Although it may not hold the status of a national holiday, April Fools' Day is widely celebrated across numerous countries annually on 1 April.

8. In Germany, a popular prank, known as "Aprilscherz", involves making up a completely fictional yet harmless story to deceive others.

9. Portuguese tradition avoids April 1st, instead choosing the Sunday and Monday before LENT for celebrations.

10. The BBC fooled their audience with a viral trailer called "Miracles of Evolution", depicting special penguins that seemingly reacquired the ability to fly.

II. Translate the following paragraph into Chinese.

The idea behind celebrating World Mother's Day is to honor the selfless love of mothers. As the popular belief goes, mothers often do not get enough credit for all the love and sacrifice that they make. Their never-ending contribution to their families in terms of love and care makes them worthy of acknowledgement and a special mention.

Therefore, International Mother's Day is a unique and friendly way to remember the spirit of motherhood and to acknowledge every motherly figure in our lives. On this day, people express their gratitude for their mothers in different ways. Considering the challenging job of a mother, from raising a child to imparting good values to them, Mother's Day is a time to celebrate the unending love of mothers towards their children. So, this occasion celebrates the sacred bond that mothers share with their children.

Cross-cultural Perspectives

Read the following paragraph and write a summary of 200 words.

●●● *Cultural Differences of Chinese and American Traditional Festival* ●●●

[1] China is a multi-ethnic nation, where different ethnic groups and regions celebrate their own unique traditional festivals. However, there are several festivals that are widely celebrated by Chinese people across the country. These include the Spring Festival, Tomb-Sweeping Day, the Dragon-Boat Festival, the ChineseValentine's Day, Mid-Autumn Day, and the Double-Ninth Festival, among others.

[2] In contrast, America is a multicultural nation, where people from various countries have come together, bringing their own cultural traditions that have blended into the distinct American culture. Festivals in America can be categorized into legal holidays, traditional festivals, and even some state-specific festivals. Some of the most popular traditional festivals celebrated by Americans include New Year's Day, Valentine's Day, April Fools' Day, Mother's Day, Father's Day, Halloween, Easter, Thanksgiving Day, and Christmas, among others.

[3] Traditional festivals are the historical products of a nation's development. Whether in China which has a long history of more than five thousand years or in the newborn America, the origins of traditional festivals share similarities. Most traditional festivals originated from people's expectation for harvest in the agricultural production, the worship towards the gods and the nature, sacrifices to the historical characters etc. After the long-term evolution, traditional festivals have become an indispensable part of the national culture. Through traditional festivals, the distinct cultural characteristics of a people and the national spirits can be observed.

Differences between Chinese and American Traditional Festivals

[4] Traditional festivals, as an integral part of the national culture, possess rich cultural connotations. It is no wonder that there are traditional festivals in the two cultures with the similar cultural connotations, such as The Spring Festival vs. Thanksgiving Day, The Zhongyuan Festival vs. Halloween. However, The Chinese Valentine's Day vs. Valentine's Day. Behind the similar cultural connotations of traditional festivals, origins and customs of these festivals are greatly differentiated, which illustrate the cultural differences of the two nations.

[5] In view of origins, the Spring Festival has close relation to agriculture. Actually, most Chinese traditional festivals are derived from people's conducting the agricultural production. Comparatively speaking, origins of American traditional festivals reflect the influence of religion, mainly Christianity. Thanksgiving Day is related to religion to some extent, although it is originated in the celebration of harvest, the influence of agriculture on this festival has faded away, and it tends to be a festival for family reunion and showing thanks to the God. In fact, among all the American traditional festivals many are originated from Christianity. There are many gods in China's legends. The Qixi Festival is rooted in the story of Cowherd and Weaver Girl who was the seventh daughter of the Jade Emperor and Queen Mother in the Heaven.

[6] In view of customs, etiquette has been greatly emphasized in celebration of Chinese traditional festivals. Take the Spring Festival for example, etiquette can be seen everywhere: the seating arrangement at the family reunion dinner, the elder giving "red envelops" to the younger, the younger giving gifts to their parents, the descendants offering sacrifices to their ancestors, people saying greetings to each other, paying New Year calls to relatives and friends with gifts. Etiquette has been regarded as a criterion to judge an individual's personality to some degree. Besides, most Chinese traditional festivals attach more importance to harmony and

happiness among people. While in America celebrations for traditional festivals are more tending to be for fun and recreation. At the same time, the customs of traditional festivals are somewhat religious, for example, the prayer before the Thanksgiving dinner, people going to the church at the Easter morning.

Main Factors of Differences between Chinese and American Traditional Festivals

[7] China is a country that bears wisdom of generations and a national history of centuries; therefore, it is inevitable for traditional festivals to go through dramatic changes for "it is a general law in human history that the various civilizations polarized, synchronized, and affected each other". In history, such factors as religion, literature and arts, Confucianism, Taoism, Buddhism from the foreign land and politics and others have exerted a significant and positive influence on the culture loaded by Chinese traditional festivals. Agricultural civilization and Confucianism are the primary ones among all the factors that have contributed to distinct characteristics of Chinese traditional festivals.

[8] The agricultural civilization is the foundation of most Chinese traditional festivals. The time system of Chinese traditional festivals is born from the system of "solar terms" because "solar terms" provide the prerequisite for deciding the time for festivals. Most festivals are celebrated around or on some solar term.

[9] Different from China, America is a highly industrialized country. With the fast pace of the industrialization in America, agricultural characteristics in the traditional festivals gradually disappear. The Thanksgiving as the festival most closely related to the agricultural production is no longer a festival to celebrate the harvest but a festival for the reunion of the family members and showing their thanks to the God. Furthermore, with the several immigration waves bringing abundant labor force for the industrialization in America, many foreign festivals have also been embedded in the system of traditional festivals in America.

[10] Religion is vital to the American people's life. The belief in Christianity is the source of formation of most American traditional festivals. Christmas is celebrated in the memory of Jesus' birth; Easter is celebrated in the memory of his resurrection. Other festivals have also been branded by Christianity, such as the Valentine's Day and the Halloween. The Valentine's Day is said to commemorate the saint Valentine, and Halloween, originally as a day to memorialize the dead, has become a day in the memory of all the saints.

[11] The differences between the Chinese and Western traditional festivals contribute to the beauty and diversity of the world. However, it is also important to acknowledge that there are similarities that exist between them. By recognizing these similarities, we can gain a more comprehensive understanding of cultural diversity and approach problems from a dialectical perspective.

Case Study

"A holiday of a nation represents a glorious culture and concentrated customs of a nation." To understand a nation's cultural implications and its cultural characteristics, we must start with its traditional festivals. There exists great difference between Chinese and Western festivals due to their different languages, education, life styles and customs. The differences in their origin and shaping, celebration, food, banquet manners, color of festive dressing and the attitudes of accepting presents contribute to the great differences of Chinese and Western festive cultures.

Western traditional festivals emphasize on interactivity, collectivity and extreme carnival, focusing on self and advocating free expressing of personality. While in China, we focus on family reunion and enjoy happy family relations. Here we set two examples as follows.

In Western nations, the New Year's Day falls on January 1st in Gregorian calendar. On the night of December 31, particularly close to the late zero o'clock, tens of thousands of people gather in to pray sincerely and silently for the coming year's countdown. When the bell sounds 12, suddenly, the beautiful music sound, people are singing happily and talking cheerfully, playing all night long.

In China, the Spring Festival falls on January 1st in lunar calendar since Qin Dynasty. On the eve of Spring Festival, we get together to enjoy delicious food and cuisine, staying up for the coming New Year to bid farewell to the old year. The whole family will spend a beautiful night in the sound of firecrackers. The Spring Festival lasts until Lantern Festival. Spring cleaning, New Year gathering, firecrackers, lion dance are the popular customs during Spring Festival. Each of the two festivals has its strong points: The Western New Year embodies fashion trend and modern life. While Chinese people attach great importance to dense national culture and traditional atmosphere to the Spring Festival; it has the glorious history and the unique beauty.

Work collaboratively in groups to produce a 5-minute video illustrating your comprehension of the similarities and differences between the Western New Year's Day and Chinese Spring Festival.

4-2　Unit 4 译文及答案

Unit 5

Wedding Customs and Ceremonies

Unit Objectives

· To acquire vocabulary and expressions related to wedding customs and ceremonies in China and the West.
· To gain a general knowledge of the characteristics of wedding customs in China and the West.
· To express informed opinions and thoughtful analysis about wedding customs.
· To develop a sense of appreciation and confidence in Chinese wedding customs.

Read and Discuss

Unit 5 Wedding Customs and Ceremonies

Read the following paragraph and discuss the following questions.

Building a human community with a shared future is the way forward for all the world's peoples. An ancient Chinese philosopher observed that "all living things may grow side by side without harming one another, and different roads may run in parallel without interfering with one another". Only when all countries pursue the cause of common good, live in harmony, and engage in cooperation for mutual benefit will there be sustained prosperity and guaranteed security. It is in this spirit that China has put forward the Global Development Initiative and the Global Security Initiative, and it stands ready to work with the international community to put these two initiatives into action.

1. What is the significance of building a human community with a shared future?

2. How does China's concept of building a human community with a shared future differ from the Western approach to international cooperation and development?

3. What similarities exist between the connotations of human community and marriage?

Section A

▼ Knowledge Focus

Ⅰ. **Fill in the blanks based on your understanding of the online video lectures.**

●●● *Customs before the Wedding in China* ●●●

From the Qin (221 BC-207 BC) to Qing (1644-1911) Dynasties, the feudal system dominated over two thousand years. In 1) _____ , a marriage would be decided not by a young couple's love, but by their parents' desires. Only after a 2) _____ and when parents considered the two families' conditions were similar and could be matched, would the marriage 3) _____ go forward. Conditions that should be taken into consideration included wealth and social status. If a boy had a rich family, his parents would never permit him to marry a girl from a poor

5-1
Customs before the
Wedding in China
扫码观看视频

family. The essentials to the marriage process were the commonly recognized 4) _____.

The Three Letters are the letter of 5) _____, the letter of gift list and the letter of marriage. The letter of betrothal is the formal document of the 6) _____, which is a must in a marriage. The letter of gift list is a list of gifts that the groom's family will send to the bride's family. The groom's family and the matchmaker will discuss what gifts should be included and then make a decision and write the names and 7) _____ on a well-decorated red paper. This is the letter of gift list. Since Chinese people think highly of 8) _____, it is a common practice for the groom's parents to try their best to send as many expensive gifts to the bride's family as possible. This also demonstrates the social position and economic condition of the groom's family. The letter of marriage is prepared and presented to the bride's family on the day of the wedding and is a document that 9) _____ of the bride into the groom's family. It serves as the marriage certificate.

While the Three Letters are crucial documents in traditional weddings, the Six Etiquettes are necessary rituals conducted in traditional wedding ceremonies, without which marriage is not 10) _____. The Six Etiquettes are nacai(纳采), wenming(问名), naji(纳吉), nazheng(纳征), qingqi(请期) and qinying(亲迎).

Ⅱ. Choose the best answer to each of the following questions.

1. Traditionally, who proposed marriage in ancient China?
   A. The young man's parents.
   B. The young man's father.
   C. The young man himself.
   D. A matchmaker.

2. What's the purpose of visiting the girls' parents according to *The Book of Rites*?
   A. To get to know who the girl's mother is.
   B. To get to know who the girl's father is.
   C. To get to know the girl's temperament.
   D. To choose a wedding date.

3. Which of the following is the most important rite initiating the preparation of a traditional Chinese wedding?
   A. Nacai.
   B. Wenming.
   C. Nazheng.
   D. Naji.

Unit 5　Wedding Customs and Ceremonies

4. Which statement about the marriage in ancient China is true?

A. The marriage is mainly about the woman and the man.

B. The marriage is between the woman and the family of her husband.

C. The marriage is very similar to the Westerners' love marriage.

D. The marriage is still legal if the bride happened to die before miaojian.

5. According to the ritual of returning to the bride's parents' home in China, which of the following statement is NOT true?

A. The bride is received as a guest rather than a hostess.

B. The groom should prepare very well and bring certain gifts.

C. The new couple can stay at the bride's parents' home for the night.

D. It is a good chance for the parents-in-law to see whether the couple will have a happy marriage.

6. What does the man customarily give to his fiancée as a symbol of the engagement in America?

A. A diamond necklace.

B. A copper bracelet.

C. A gold ring.

D. A diamond ring.

7. Why does the groom have a "best man" to stand beside him and help him during the wedding ceremony?

A. Because he could help the groom avoid drinking too much.

B. Because he could help the groom intimidate the maid.

C. Because he could help the groom escape from the bride's father.

D. Because he could help the groom relax and enjoy the reception.

8. Which of the following statements about the American wedding ceremony is NOT true?

A. It is bad luck for the bride and groom to see each other before the wedding.

B. Wearing something old is considered to bring good luck to the marriage.

C. Wearing something borrowed can bring lasting happiness to brides' marriage.

D. Wearing something white means purity, fidelity and love.

9. Customarily, who will enter last in the wedding march?

A. The groom.

B. The bride and her father.

C. The maids.

D. The flower girls.

10. Which explanation about the custom of tossing the bouquet in American weddings is true?

A. The person who catches the bouquet is believed to be the next one to get married.

B. The person who catches the bouquet is expected to make a speech.

C. The person who catches the bouquet will receive a gift from the bride and groom.

D. The person who catches the bouquet will simply feel happy about participating in the tradition.

Ⅲ. Decide whether each of the following statements is true (T) or false (F).

1. If the Eight Characters of Birth of the boy and the girl are compatible, according to *The Book of Changes*, they will lead a happy life and will help and bring good luck to each other.

2. The couple's zodiac signs have no influence on choosing an auspicious wedding date.

3. The groom is always accompanied by a wedding procession when picking up the bride in qinying.

4. The ritual of miaojian usually begins by the father of the groom or the senior member of the family. He should kneel down before the ancestral altar to announce to the spirits of the dead ancestors that a descendant of the family has now brought a wife home and the family will be booming.

5. In the past, the appellation of the woman changes depending on the number of children she has.

6. Groom's Stag Party is a celebration for the bride-to-be's last night of freedom, involving both men and women.

7. Rehearsal dinners are usually sponsored by the bride's family as a thanksgiving meal to the wedding entourage.

8. Engaged couples in America often receive counseling to prepare for married life.

9. The wedding ring is worn on the third finger of the left hand.

10. The tradition of honeymooning is related to the custom of drinking mead and honey during the first thirty days of marriage.

Language Focus

I. **Match the words and definitions.**

____auspicious   ____banter   ____betrothal   ____civic
____descendant   ____embodiment   ____foreshadow   ____integral
____obedient   ____superstitious

A. the people in later generations who are related to them
B. an agreement to marry somebody
C. a person or thing that represents or is a typical example of an idea or a quality
D. being an essential part of something
E. showing signs that something is likely to be successful in the future
F. believing in superstitions
G. doing what you are told to do; willing to obey
H. connected with the people who live in a town or city
I. to be a sign of something that will happen in the future
J. to joke with somebody

II. There are 10 errors altogether in the following paragraph(s). The errors are: missing words, unnecessary words and wrong words. Please correct them as follows: for a missing word, mark its position with the symbol "∧" and write it; for an unnecessary word, cross it out with the symbol "\"; for a wrong word, underline it and write the correct word.

On the wedding day, when the guests arrive for a wedding ceremony, the ushers' duty is to insure the guests are seated in the correct places. Traditionally, the side on that people	1. _____ 2. _____

sit depends on whether they are friends or families of the bride or of the groom. The front row are generally reserved for close families or friends, and the very first seats reserved for close families or friends, with the very first seats reserve for the bridal party. However, in many ceremonies the bridal party will remain stand at the altar during the ceremony along with the bride and groom. The groom and his best man wait for inside the church for the arrival of the bride and her entourage. This entourage general arrives in elegant cars or in horse-drawn coaches, specially hired for an occasion. The bride's entourage normally consists the bride, the bride's father and all the bridesmaids, maids of honor, flower girls.

3. _____

4. _____

5. _____

6. _____

7. _____

8. _____

9. _____

10. _____

Critical Thinking

Discuss the following questions in small groups and share your ideas in class.

1. What are the unique national characteristics of Chinese and American wedding ceremony?

2. What are the overall impressions Chinese and American wedding ceremonies leave on people?

3. What are people's perceptions on marriage in China and America?

4. What are the differences in the criteria of selecting a spouse between Chinese and Americans?

5. How do the different philosophic thoughts of Chinese and Americans shape their wedding customs?

6. Compared with the traditional wedding customs in China, is there any change of these customs? If yes, what are they?

Case Study

A young American recently posed the question on Quora: Why do Chinese people place such high value on marriage? It is often observed that parents in Chinese culture prioritize their adult children getting married, even if it means marrying someone their children may not necessarily like.

If you were invited to share your opinion on this question on Quora, what comments would you make?

Section B

Passage 1

Bride Price Tradition Fueling Fresh Friction

[A] The practice of giving money as a wedding guarantee comes under scrutiny as amounts skyrocket.

[B] The recent break-up of a prospective bride and groom as a result of a failure to agree on a bride price of 300,000 yuan has caused heated debate online nationwide. A bride price is the cash sum a prospective groom pays to the family of his wife-to-be as a guarantee that he will marry her and will treat her well in the future. The practice is legal, but the sums demanded in some parts of the country have risen dramatically in recent years as some families want to test the depth of feeling the groom's parents have toward the prospective newcomer to their household.

[C] In April, the prospective groom, from Zhengning county, Gansu province, wrote on a government message board that he almost married his girlfriend, but the high bride price demanded by her parents "forced" the couple to break up. He said he hoped the government would rectify the trend of rising bride prices. In reply, the Party committee office of Zhengning said the county government had already issued a guideline advocating that the bride price for rural marriages should not exceed 80,000 yuan, but stipulated that government officials should set an example by asking for less than 60,000 yuan. It added that there is a long way to go before what it called "the old, bad social tradition" is abandoned.

[D] The news sparked concerns among netizens who were thinking of getting married. Many left comments under the post, with the most popular saying that the best thing to do is to avoid marriage altogether.

[E] Zhang Furong, who owns a marriage agency in Xichang, Sichuan province, said that she witnessed the failure of an engagement in 2018 as a result of a high bride price. Having matched a couple, she said they had a good relationship and were discussing marriage. The woman's family asked for a bride price of 168,000 yuan because the mother said her daughter was the prettiest young woman in the neighborhood and she had a stable job as a middle school teacher. Also, a neighbor's daughter had received the same sum, so the family didn't want to appear inferior. The groom-to-be agreed to the sum, but said his family could only pay in installments because his parents had just made a 400,000 yuan down payment on a house and had also paid about 200,000 yuan for a car to help him care for his new wife. "The woman's family would not agree with the idea of paying in stages, so negotiations broke down. As the matchmaker, I was at the scene. I saw the man stand up immediately after the refusal and walk out without looking back," Zhang said. Later, the woman's mother called Zhang to say that she regretted her actions and wanted to save her daughter's marriage prospects. The mother added that she didn't mean to "sell" her daughter, but she had "lost her mind" during the negotiations on an impulse to compete with her neighbor. In the end, the couple parted for good, so Zhang helped them find new partners. The mother lowered the bride price by 50 percent and her daughter married quickly. Both parties are now married and have children.

[F] "In my opinion, they were really suited to each other, so I was sorry they broke up. Maybe they were not meant to be a couple," Zhang said.

From gifts to cash

[G] The tradition of giving a bride price in the form of gifts has existed for thousands of years. In return, the family of the prospective bride must pay for the engagement and give a lump sum as a dowry.

[H] In modern China, the bilateral payments have developed from gifts to cash. For couples from families of comparable financial status, the bride's parents usually give a dowry of almost the same amount as the bride price. The combined cash is used to help the newlyweds start their life together. However, in some small cities and counties, many young women tend to move to big cities for work. That results in an excess of males of marriageable age, meaning that bride prices are generally higher while dowries are smaller.

[I] DengYaju has been a matchmaker for two years in Zhengning, the county that hit the headlines recently. She said that young men in Zhengning are less demanding because after several unsatisfactory blind dates they realize that it is difficult to find the right partner. "By contrast, young women in these places usually aim high, especially those who have returned to the county after working in big cities," she said. "As they have received more education, seen more of the world and can earn more money, they are pickier about prospective partners, which raises the bride price." Deng said the high bride price locally is also due to women's desire to compare themselves to others. If a woman gets a lower bride price than her peers, people around her may think that there is something wrong with her. In some poor families that contain both a son and daughter, the parents ask for a high bride price because they want to give the money to their son to help him find a wife. Some families even fall into debt after paying the bride price. Now, the trend is being reversed as governments at all levels are advocating cheaper wedding ceremonies and reasonable bride prices.

Sustainable approach

[J] Meanwhile, the younger generation of couples is pursuing a more sustainable way of marriage.

[K] He Fan, a 24-year-old newlywed from Weifang, Shandong province, received a bride price of 100,000 yuan, but returned 80,000 yuan as her dowry. Her 25-year-old husband lives in the province's Zaozhuang. He works as a programmer, earning 7,000 yuan a month. He has a car, but owns no property. "My husband and I met online while playing the same games. I trust him and I don't need money to prove his love to me," She said, "My parents had a good first impression of him, but they needed him to show good faith in the marriage via the bride price because they were worried that I might be wronged by my new family." She said her bride price was much lower than the local average, but her parents still agreed to the marriage and returned 80 percent as a dowry to help support the newlyweds. "I like him, not his bride price. A happy marriage is more important than a high bride price, which is just a formality," She said.

[L] In a video she posted in April, Yang Shuhui, a 27-year-old video blogger from Zhejiang province who has millions of followers on social media, gave her thoughts on bride price as she announced that she was getting married. "In big cities it's true that people in their 20s really can't afford to buy a house, so they need the starting capital as help from parents," she said, adding that young people and parents are trying to achieve a balance.

I. Fast reading.

Direction: Each statement of the following contains information given in one of the paragraphs in the above passage. Identify the paragraph from which the information is derived. You may choose a paragraph more than once. Each paragraph is marked with a letter.

1. A woman who runs a marriage agency has witnessed an engagement failure due to a substantial bride price.

2. Giving money as a wedding guarantee is under scrutiny because of the sharp increase of amounts of the money.

3. In some cities, the bride prices are generally higher because of a surplus of males of marriageable age.

4. Some netizens hold that the best thing to do is to avoid marriage.

5. A recent break-up of a couple-to-be as a result of the disagreement over the bride price has aroused heated discussions among Chinese netizens.

6. According to a video blogger, young people desperately need financial assistance from parents because they can't afford to buy a house in big cities.

7. The locally high bride price can also be attributed to women's desire to compare themselves with peers.

8. A groom-to-be from Gansu province suggested online that the government should rectify the trend of rising bride prices.

9. The tradition of giving a bride price and a dowry has existed for thousands of years in China.

10. A bride-to-be believes that a happy marriage holds greater significance than a lofty bride price, which is merely a formality.

Ⅱ. Translate the following paragraph into English.

中国传统婚礼是华夏文化的重要部分。中国古人通常会在黄昏举行婚礼，因为古人认为黄昏是一天中最吉利的时刻。中国人喜爱红色，红色象征着幸福、成功、好运、忠诚和繁荣。因此，在传统中国婚礼上，主色调是红色，有红色的蜡烛、红色的缎带、红花、红色衣服和红鞋。新娘吃的食物也是一种文化象征。新娘一般会吃红枣、花生、桂圆和瓜子，其中的象征意义可以从这四种食物的读音中看出。当这四种食物放在一起读时就是"早生贵子"。

Passage 2

∙∙∙ *Six Things to Ask Yourself before Getting Married* ∙∙∙

[1] Millions of divorces take place all around the world every year. Many of them happen because one of the partners has changed significantly. Some of them happen because of the chronic cheating habits of either partner. But most of them happen because they were not in the right marriage to begin with. Those marriages took place because the partners didn't (or couldn't) give as much thought to their decision (of getting married) as they should have. They didn't ask the right questions. They weren't ready for the right evaluations (of themselves and their partners) and couldn't anticipate the profound change that marriage would bring to their lives.

[2] Are you thinking of getting married? In that case, have you made a careful assessment of your relationship to check if it is marriage-ready? If not, here are the six crucial questions that you must ask yourselves before you pop the question. While there are many more factors specific to your relationship which you can (and should) take into account, make sure you don't miss out on these six.

1. Are our life and career goals similar?

[3] Marriage is a decision to inextricably join your life with someone else. Aligning your life, career and other important goals is crucial.

[4] Do you want to settle down in a quaint suburb and have lots of kids? Then don't marry someone who wants to live and work in five continents. Are you planning to pool all your resources, throw them (and yourself) head-on into your new start-up— the dream of your life? Then don't marry someone who wants a stable, cushy life and lots of "quality time" together.

2. Do we fulfill each other's needs?

[5] We all have emotional, intellectual, physical, practical, social and various other needs from a relationship. If you're in a relationship and are planning to get married, ask yourself— have you made a rational, clear-headed evaluation of whether and how much of your needs your significant other fulfills? Or are you glossing over your unfulfilled needs thinking "every relationship requires compromise"? This is important because when we're in the throes of that addictive drug called love, we tend to see only positives in the person we're in love with.

[6] Now nothing can be truer than the fact that every relationship takes some ceding of grounds, and kudos to you if you're willingly doing your bit. But if you ignore your basic needs,

they will find a way to come back to you in the long run— in the form of fights, emotional abuse, cheating and even divorce.

3. Do we really know each other?

[7] I was once with a guy who lied about his age on Facebook, and I never asked him about it. We were six months into the relationship when I discovered he was five years older than I thought. Yes, you guessed it— that was not the only lie on which the relationship was based. No wonder we didn't stay together much more than a year.

[8] Knowing your partner and allowing him/her to know you are vital aspects of a stable relationship. Trust takes an immense amount of work (and time) to build, but only seconds to lose. Be honest and tell your partner everything you think he or she should know about you. This will make it easier for him/her to do the same.

[9] Needless to say, if you can't trust your partner enough to do that, it is probably not the time to think about marriage.

4. Do we know how to deal with each other's "negative" sides?

[10] You can't live without your dogs. But your girlfriend would rather die than live with them. You're a devil incarnate when you're angry. You're struggling with a bad spending habit. We all have our negative aspects. If you're thinking about making a lifelong commitment to someone it's crucial to understand and develop strategies to deal with each other's less-than-desirable traits. Make a conscious decision to go (or not to go) pet-less for the rest of your life for a partner who's allergic to your pets. Make your peace with the problematic spending habits of your significant other before you decide to take the plunge.

[11] It takes time to understand and deal with things we don't like about our partners. And until and unless you've spent that time, you're not ready to make a decision on marriage.

5. Do we admire and respect each other?

[12] Intelligence? Simplicity? A caring heart? A strong common interest? Is there something in him/her which genuinely complements you in ways more than one? Falling in love with someone "for no particular reason" is great for the heady period of infatuation but not nearly enough for the everyday reality of marriage. Ask yourselves whether you admire each other for the special individuals that you are and the unique qualities that you both possess.

[13] Marriage is a long— sometimes boring, but stable— commitment. It cannot be based on whether someone is exciting to you. It has to be about finding long-term fulfillment and happiness in the individuals that you are.

6. Am I ready to think of him/her as a parent of my children?

[14] You love your partner like mad? Great. But do you also respect them? Are you proud

of him/her? Remember, your legacy to this world will be as much a part of you as of him/her. Unless it fills your heart with joy to think of him/her as a parent of your child, you should probably think about that marriage thing again. In this regard it's important to take not only your significant other, but also their family into account. Your child will carry as much of your genes as theirs. Is that something that makes you happy?

[15] Marriage is a decision that will change your life, one way or the other. Keeping a few basic principles in mind and asking the right questions will make sure you steer clear of pitfalls that often contribute to divorce.

I. Answer the following questions.

1. Why do millions of divorces take place all around the world every year?

2. Why should we make rational, clear-headed evaluations of whether and how much of your needs our significant others fulfill?

3. In the eyes of the author, what does "really know each other" mean?

4. What is important for the everyday reality of a marriage?

5. Why should we ask ourselves whether we're ready to think of him/her as a parent of our child?

II. Translate the following paragraph into Chinese.

Although most American weddings follow long-standing traditions, the pursuit of individualism is also fully reflected in their weddings. For example, the usual place for a wedding is in a church. But some Americans get married outdoors in a scenic spot. A few even have the ceremony while skydiving or riding on horseback! The couple may invite hundreds of people or just a few close friends. During the ceremony they choose colors, decorations, and music that represent their own styles. However, some things rarely change. The bride usually wears a beautiful, long white wedding gown. She customarily wears "something old, something new, something borrowed and something blue", while the groom dresses in a formal suit or tuxedo.

Cross-cultural Perspectives

Read the following paragraph and write a summary of 200 words.

Comparative Analysis of the Attitudes toward Marriage in Chinese and Western Cultures

[1] When referring to the marriage customs, it is of both practical and theoretical significance to explore the cultural origins so as to help the cultural exchange. When summing up the researches concerning about it, a lot of scholars have made great efforts on marriage customs from the perspectives of values, beliefs, the gods of marriage, etc. However, the researches are all the analysis of the cultural differences from the surface so some deeper studies still need to be done. As what is said by Samovar, "It is the deep structure that unifies a culture, makes each culture unique, and explains how and why behind a culture's collective action". Therefore, this paper will try to explore the cultural origins from the perspectives of philosophy so as to have a deeper understanding.

Attitudes towards marriage in Chinese and western cultures

[2] The different attitudes towards marriage in Chinese and western cultures can be illustrated by the following analysis.

The intentions of marriage

[3] In the eyes of Chinese and westerners, the intentions of marriage are different. In traditional Chinese's opinions, they get married mainly for two reasons: One is to have offspring and the other is to consolidate the benefits of the families. Nowadays the intentions of marriage in China have changed a lot. Although the reproductive function is still being stressed, people tend to attach more attention on the functions of supporting and accompanying. From the point of view of westerners, marriage also has two intentions: One is to give a good result of their love and the other one is to find a life-long partner so as to be fulfilled physiologically and psychologically. That is to say, the reason for westerners is to find a beloved one so that they can share their life and support each other. In general, Chinese marriage is an obligation to the family, while western marriage is the personal right.

The standards of choosing a spouse

[4] Due to the differences in the intentions of marriage, Chinese and westerners differ in

the standards of choosing a spouse. For traditional Chinese people, the social rank of the family and the virtues of the girl are the most important factors. While in modern China, these two principles have weakened in the influence as more elements should be thought about, but the economic condition, family background and the virtues are still the elements that should be taken into consideration at the first place, and then are the elements of education and appearance. Thus love is not necessary in a Chinese marriage. However, westerners are quite different in choosing a spouse. For them, love is the priority in a marriage. The compatibility of the two persons is enough for their marriage. Therefore, other elements like family background, economic condition and education can be ignored.

The relationship of husband and wife in a marriage

[5] In traditional Chinese people's views, husband is the head of a family and the wife must rely on him or she will have no money to live on. Therefore, the relationship between them is unequal. Now the wife's position has been improved in modern China and many wives have the jobs to support themselves. However, in many cases, Chinese wives still like to depend on their husbands. While in the west, the relationship between the husband and wife are to some extent equal as they must perform each one's rights and obligations. In the book *An Introduction to American Culture*, Maryanne, Crandall and Kearny write that "the husband and wife should be equal partners". This can be seen in the daily life. The husband and wife both share the responsibilities of making money, doing housework, taking care of the children and cooking the meal, which are the signs of equality.

Philosophic analysis

[6] Marriage, as one of the most important parts in a person's life, is always the theme in philosophy. People's philosophic thoughts in various cultures about marriage help cultivate the diverse values so different marriage customs gradually come into being.

Chinese Confucian philosophic views

[7] The attitudes towards marriage in China are mainly influenced by Confucianism as it is the dominated political ideas in Chinese history for thousands of years. Generally speaking, Confucianism has the following views of marriage.

[8] For Confucian, it is natural to get married. Mencius once said, "The desire for food and sex is part of human nature". In their views, everything can be divided into yin and yang. For example, heaven and men are yang, while earth and women are yin. The sympathetic harmony of yin and yang, which creates the world, is a natural thing. So is the marriage between men and women. Therefore, getting married so as to have babies is an unalterable principle in Confucianism, and if someone does not follow this rule, he/she will be blamed by the society. Due to this point of view, Chinese people highlight the intention of reproducing offspring in a

marriage, which can be seen in the customs. People use the Chinese pronunciations of "red jujube", "peanut", "longan" and "lotus seed" to wish the newly-married couple to have earthly birth of babies.

Marriage made in heaven

[9] Marriage is made in heaven in Confucianism. That is to say, the spouses have been decided by destiny, so the only way is to accept it. Therefore, although the men and women have no specially feelings with each other, they have to get married under the pressure of the society. Even if they are not happy in the married life, they will try to stand the heaven-made marriage. Due to this reason, marriage in China is very stable. In the wedding ceremony, the worship of heaven and earth by the bride and the bridegroom at the very beginning is the case in point.

Filial piety

[10] Confucianism stresses on the importance of filial piety, which may be the origin of arranged marriage. Parents are the high authority in a family so the children must respect and obey them, or they will be scolded as unfilial. Therefore, parents are in charge of their children's everything, not alone marriage. In this case, the young have little right in choosing their beloved ones, but have to marry for the command of their parents so as to meet the family's needs. Due to this reason, some people will give up their lovers and accept the marriages that made by their parents so as to please them. Besides the choosing of a spouse, filial piety also gets revealed in the wedding procedures. On the wedding ceremony, the bride and the bridegroom show thanks to their parents, and after the wedding, they have to go back to the bride's home to meet her family, which are the signs of filial piety.

The concept of family

[11] Confucianism, emphasizing on the grand unification, holds to the principle that the national interests and group benefits always come first. Due to this reason, family as the most common group is listed in the first place. In a family, the members must obey the family rules and rely on each other with the purpose to achieve the harmonious relationships among family members and win benefits for the family. Due to this reason, marriage in Confucian's view becomes a tool to bind families together so as to consolidate the social status. Therefore, people pay great attention to the choosing of spouses for their children. Apart from that, the concept of family can be implied in the wedding procedures. After the wedding, the bride must meet the family members and relatives of the bridegroom's family so as to be formally confirmed the as the daughter-in-law. And likewise, it is necessary and essential for the bridegroom to go to the bride's home on the third day after the wedding with the purpose to get a formal confirmation as the son-in-law by the bride's family. In this case, the two families set up the kinship.

The relationship between husband and wife

[12] In Confucianism, there is a saying that a virtuous woman is supposed to uphold "three obediences": be subordinate to her father before marriage, to her husband after marriage, and to her son after the death of her husband, which lays the foundation of the positions of husband and wife in a marriage. Men could remarry and have concubines, whereas women were supposed to uphold the virtue of chastity when they lost their husbands. This opinion leads to women's poor position in Chinese marriage that they have to obey and rely on their husband. Nowadays although women's position has been greatly improved and most women have jobs to support themselves, the situation still gets little changed. Men are always the master in a family.

Western philosophic views

[13] In western philosophy, marriage is always accompanied with love. From ancient Greek, the philosophers begin to think on this issue. Plato is the first scholar to begin the thinking of love. In his opinion, love is a spiritual process to the searching of the true, the good and the beauty. Grabbing the rationality of human nature, he thinks love is a spiritual craziness. In his illustrations, there are three points. Firstly, the object of love is the good. It can be understood as love is a desire to seek for the good and the beauty. Secondly, the highest love is a kind of philosophy. Love is not the combination of a spouse in the sex, but is the firm and amazing bond of the soul and "the eternal knowledge" which far exceeds sex. Thirdly, love is to seek for the deficiencies in one's characters. The desires for making up one's deficiencies push people on their way to love. Although Plato highlights the rationality in life, he does not deny the sex. He thinks people should control their physical needs properly in love so as to live a happier life. Contrary to his teacher Plato, Aristotle put the physical needs of human being in the first place instead of the spiritual love. In his opinion, love originates from the desires for sex so as to meet the physical needs. However, meanwhile he also emphasizes the influence of soul to love.

[14] Plato and Aristotle's explorations of love's nature lay the foundation of the importance of love in westerner's marriage. Gradually, they relate love with marriage and put forward that love is the base of marriage. Love is not equal to marriage, and vice versa. In human history, marriage appears much earlier than love, but people do not relate them together and they do not discuss the positions and functions that love play in a marriage. It is the French philosopher Jean Meslier that first comes up with the idea that a marriage without love is immoral. Later, Hegel illustrates that the meaning of marriage is a law of ethics love. Then German philosopher Feuerbach states that the love between men and women is the foundation of marriage. In this way, the meaning of love gets sublimated and people find love a final place to stay-marriage. In the west, a marriage with love is a true marriage. Western philosophic views of marriage and love have huge influence on the choosing of spouses in their life so the westerners will marry to their

beloved ones and they enjoy both love and sex after marriage. A case in point is that they will choose to have a honeymoon after the wedding ceremony so as to enjoy the lover's world.

[15] People's viewpoints of marriage and love can affect their value. Chinese Confucian thoughts regard marriage as a kind of responsibility so love is not necessary the key point in it. However, western philosophic views have a long historical origin of love from ancient Greek that love can be never ignored in people's life. So it is natural for them to firmly bond marriage with love.

Case Study

According to *China Youth Daily* in 2009, several teachers and students of Nankai University completed an interesting survey. They selected some spouse-seeking advertisements in Tianjin and Boston's local mainstream newspapers to study the differences of selecting a spouse in these two cities. The survey showed that the words and sentences often appeared in men's advertisements in Tianjin newspaper were "have a stable job", "no bad habits" and "responsible"; and women's advertisements always emphasized that they were kind, virtuous and from a good family; while in Boston, both men and women would indicate their races, religious beliefs and hobbies, they would say they loved sports, they were smart and had a sense of humor.

Work collaboratively in groups to produce a 5-minute video illustrating what you value much when you select a spouse and what contributes to the difference of spouse-seeking in China and America.

5-2　Unit 5 译文及答案

Unit 6
Music and Instruments

Unit Objectives

· To acquire vocabulary and expressions related to music in China and the West.

· To gain a general knowledge of different music styles and instruments in China and the West.

· To express informed opinions and thoughtful analysis about music.

· To develop a sense of appreciation and confidence in Chinese music.

Read and Discuss

Read the following paragraph and discuss the following questions.

Build cultural confidence and strength and secure new successes in developing socialist culture. We will develop a sound, people-oriented socialist culture for our nation that embraces modernization, the world, and the future. We will ignite the cultural creativity of the entire nation and build a powerful source of inspiration for realizing national rejuvenation. We should uphold the foundational system for ensuring the guiding role of Marxism in the ideological domain. We will ensure that culture serves the people and serves socialism. We will follow the principle of letting a hundred flowers bloom and a hundred schools of thought contend, and we will encourage creative transformation and innovative development of traditional Chinese culture.

1. What does the principle of letting a hundred flowers bloom and a hundred schools of thought contend mean for the development of China's music industry?
_____

2. How can the cultural creativity of the entire nation contribute to the development of China's music industry?
_____

3. How can traditional Chinese music and instruments be creatively transformed to reflect contemporary interests and tastes?
_____

Section A

▼ Knowledge Focus

Ⅰ. Fill in the blanks based on your understanding of the online video lectures.

••• Peking Opera •••

Peking Opera is one of the most remarkable and famous opera styles. It arose in the late 18th century and became fully developed and 1)_____ by the 19th century. Like many other traditional Chinese operas, Peking Opera mainly relies on singing and dancing to tell stories. Its performers use four basic performing methods on stage: singing, 2)_____, acting, and combats. Their gestures and movements are often 3)_____ rather than realistic. Above all else, the skill of the performer is evaluated according to the beauty of their movements.

Peking Opera features four main types of roles—Sheng, the major male characters; Dan, the female roles; Jing, the characters with the most colorful faces; and Chou, the ugly and 4) _____ roles. Each actor is usually good at portraying at least one of these roles. Due to the long distance and frequent traveling of the opera troupes, the Dan role, which 5) _____ female character, used to be performed by male actors. For instance, Mei Lanfang, one of the famous Peking Opera actors, was known for his performance of Dan role. He successfully created various images of ancient Chinese women and expressed their 6) _____. Moreover, Mei Lanfang was also the first person to introduce Peking Opera to foreign countries and he won international honors for his art.

The Peking Opera band mainly consists of 7) _____ and a percussion band. The former frequently accompanies peaceful scenes while the latter provides the exciting atmosphere for battle scenes. The most important musical instrument used for the Peking Opera is jinghu, a kind of two-stringed fiddle, followed by erhu, also a two-stringed fiddle but 8) _____. These string instruments are often used when playing for peaceful scenes. Other instruments include yueqin, pipa, etc. The percussion instruments are gongs and drums of different sizes, and castanets made of 9) _____. The castanets play an important role in making the tempo; they are the "time-beater", and the whole orchestra is virtually directed by them. With the aid of gongs and drums, they 10) _____ for the actor, regulate his/her motions, and give the performers cues.

Ⅱ. Choose the best answer to each of the following questions.

1. What is Chinese Opera recognized as in terms of ancient Chinese art forms?

   A. A unique and supreme example of theatre show.

   B. A popular music genre in China.

   C. A modern form of entertainment.

   D. A type of dance performance.

2. Which of the following statements about traditional Chinese musical instruments is NOT true?

   A. The zither has a long history and is known as the "instrument of the sages".

   B. Many well-known writers and poets created poems and mentioned pipa in their works.

   C. The horse-headed fiddle is a bowed stringed-instrument with a scroll carved like a horse's head, and it is popular in Mongolian music.

   D. The erhu was an important instrument when playing for peaceful scenes.

3. What was the name of the first known opera troupe in China, founded by Emperor TangXuanzong?

   A. Golden Palace.

   B. Jade Garden.

C. Silk Road.

D. Pear Garden.

4. Who used to perform the Dan role in Peking Opera?

A. Female actors.

B. Male actors.

C. Opera singers.

D. Acrobats.

5. What is the meaning of the famous guqin music "Lofty Mountains and Flowing Water"?

A. The natural scenery of lofty mountains and flowing water.

B. The sadness of losing a friend.

C. The joy of spring and new beginnings.

D. The importance of true friendship.

6. Which of the following statements about Country Music is NOT true?

A. It originates from the British Isles, church music and African American blues.

B. It has incorporated jazz, rock and roll, Mexican and Hawaiian music nowadays.

C. It was played on instruments like acoustic guitar, mandolin, autoharp, fiddle and the banjo.

D. It couldn't represent a true American sound since it has changed as time goes by.

7. What instruments were commonly used in the early development of Country Music?

A. Piano and drums.

B. Electric guitar and bass.

C. Acoustic guitar and mandolin.

D. Saxophone and trumpet.

8. Which musician began mixing elements of Country Music into his Folk Rock sound in the mid-60s?

A. Elvis Presley.

B. Carl Perkins.

C. Bob Dylan.

D. Roy Orbison.

9. Which musical genre was NOT mentioned as a style developed from Country Music?

A. Jazz.

B. Western Swing.

C. Rockabilly.

D. Country Pop.

10. What is not emphasized as one of the reasons for the continuous vitality of Country Music?

A. Adding new elements.

B. Singing about real lives.

C. Keeping up with the young generation.

D. Adhering to traditional styles.

Ⅲ. **Decide whether each of the following statements is true (T) or false (F).**

1. The Chinese contemporary music market is primarily filled with traditional Chinese music styles.

2. Most operas were composed according to the ancient novels, which have not benefited from the operas.

3. The saying "One minute's performance on the stage takes ten years' practice behind the scenes" reflects the dedication and hard work required in Chinese opera.

4. During the Ming Dynasty, qu, one type of literature based on music became popular.

5. Yu Boya and Zhong Ziqi were good friends who enjoyed playing music together.

6. Country Music remained as one of the few truly indigenous American musical styles into the late 20th century.

7. Taylor Swift is known for singing about the lives of other people.

8. Nowadays, Country Music singers continue to develop it with popular musical styles and various themes.

9. Wuhan Qintai Grand Theatre represents only the modern development of Chinese music industry.

10. The protest song *Blowing in the Wind* was written by Elvis Presley.

Language Focus

Ⅰ. Match the words and definitions.

____ acrobat   ____ duplicity   ____ emulate   ____ genre
____ orchestra ____ outlaw   ____ percussion ____ refinement
                ____ troupe   ____ vocal

A. a small change to something that improves it

B. (used especially about people in the past) a person who has done something illegal and is hiding to avoid being caught

C. a particular type or style of literature, art, film or music that you can recognize because of its special features

D. musical instruments that you play by hitting them with your hand or with a stick, for example drums

E. a group of actors, singers, etc. who work together

F. connected with the voice

G. a large group of people who play various musical instruments together, led by a conductor

H. dishonest behavior that is intended to make somebody believe something which is not true

I. to try to do something as well as somebody else because you admire them

J. an entertainer who performs difficult acts such as balancing on high ropes, especially at a circus

Ⅱ. There are 10 errors altogether in the following paragraph(s). The errors are: missing words, unnecessary words and wrong words. Please correct them as follows: for a missing word, mark its position with the symbol "∧" and write it; for an unnecessary word, cross it out with the symbol "\"; for a wrong word, underline it and write the correct word.

The Peking Opera band mainly consist of an orchestra and a percussion band. The former frequent accompanies peaceful scenes	1. _____ 2. _____

since the latter provides the exciting atmosphere for battle scenes. The most important music instrument used for the Peking Opera is jinghu, a kind of two-stringed fiddle, following by erhu, also a two-stringed fiddle but in soft tune. These string instruments are often used when playing for peaceful scene. Other instruments include yueqin, pipa, etc. The percussion instruments are gongs and drums of different sizes, and castanets make of wood and bamboo. The castanets play an important role in making the tempo; they are the "time-beater", and for the whole orchestra is virtually directed by them. With the aid of gongs and drums, their beat time for the actor, regulate his/her motions, and give the performers cues.

3. _____
4. _____
5. _____
6. _____
7. _____
8. _____
9. _____
10. _____

▼ Critical Thinking

Discuss the following questions in small groups and share your ideas in class.

1. What is the significance of Peking Opera in Chinese culture?

2. How does the performing style in Peking Opera differ from Western opera?

3. What roles do both Peking Opera and Western opera play in the modern society?

4. What can we infer about the cultural significance and global influence of Peking Opera and Western Opera?

5. Why are Peking Opera and Western Opera considered important cultural treasures in their respective societies?

6. How can innovation and modernization be incorporated into Peking Opera without compromising its essence?

Case Study

The Divine Damsel of Devastation is an opera song featured in the game Genshin Impact. After its release, many fans uploaded their own covers of the song online. Surprisingly, many professional opera singers also joined this carnival and recreated the song. What is even more astonishing is that this song has not only captured the hearts of many young people and foreigners, but also inspired foreigners to start learning Peking Opera after hearing it. In light of this, you are supposed to write an essay analyzing the reasons behind the widespread popularity of *The Divine Damsel of Devastation* both domestically and internationally. Additionally, please introduce a specific genre of Peking Opera to foreigners and provide them with background information about this traditional art form.

In light of this, you are supposed to write an essay analyzing the reasons behind the widespread popularity of *The Divine Damsel of Devastation* both domestically and internationally. Additionally, please introduce a specific genre of Peking Opera to foreigners and provide them with background information about this traditional art form.

Section B

Passage 1

●●● Chinese Music ●●●

[A] Traditional Chinese music can be traced back 7,000-8,000 years based on the discovery of a bone flute made in the Neolithic Age. In the Xia, Shang and Zhou Dynasties, only royal families and dignitary officials enjoyed music, which was made on chimes and bells. During the Tang Dynasty, dancing and singing entered the mainstream, spreading from the royal court to the common people. With the introduction of foreign religions such as Buddhism and Islam, exotic and religious melodies were absorbed into Chinese music and were enjoyed by the Chinese people at fairs organized by religious temples.

[B] In the Song Dynasty, original opera such as Zaju and Nanxi was performed in tearooms, theatres, and showplaces. Writers and artists liked it so much that Ci, a new type of literature resembling lyrics, thrived. During the Yuan Dynasty, qu, another type of literature based on music became popular. This was also a period when many traditional musical instruments were developed such as the pipa, the flute, and the zither.

[C] During the Ming (1368-1644) and Qing Dynasties (1644-1911), the art of traditional opera developed rapidly and diversely in different regions. When these distinctive opera styles were performed at the capital (now called Beijing), artists combined the essence of the different styles and created Beijing Opera, one of three cornerstones of Chinese culture (the other two being Chinese medicine and traditional Chinese painting) which continue to be appreciated even in modern times.

[D] Besides these types of music, Chinese peasants were clever enough to compose folk songs, which also developed independently with local flavor. Folk songs described working and daily life such as fishing, farming, and herding and were very popular among the common people.

Traditional musical instruments

[E] Traditional Chinese musical instruments can be divided into four categories: stringed instruments, percussion instruments, plucked instruments, and wind instruments. The following are just a few of them.

Horse-headed fiddle

[F] The Horse-headed fiddle is a bowed stringed-instrument with a scroll carved like a horse's head. It is popular in Mongolian music. With a history of over 1,300 years, it even influenced European string music when Marco Polo brought one back from his travels through Asia. Its wide tonal range and deep, hazy tone color express the joy or pathos of a melody to its fullest.

[G] The Mongolian people bestowed upon their beloved horse-headed fiddle a fantastic legend: during horse-racing at the Nadam Fair— their featured grand festival— a hero, Su He, and his white horse ran the fastest, which incurred the envy and wrath of the duke. The cruel duke shot the horse dead, and Su He grieved so much that he met his horse in a dream. In the dream, the horse told Su He to make a fiddle from wood and the hair of a horse's tail, and to carve the head of the fiddle in the shape of a horse's head. The lad followed the horse's advice and when he finished, the fiddle produced an extremely vivid sound. From then on, people loved this instrument and composed many songs for it.

Lute (Pipa)

[H] Originally named after the loquat fruit, the earliest pipa known was found to have been made in the Qin Dynasty (221 BC-207 BC). By the Tang Dynasty (618-907), the pipa had reached its summit. It was loved by everyone—from the royal court to the common folk—and it occupied the predominant place in the orchestra. Many well-known writers and poets created poems and mentioned it in their works. Bai Juyi, the master poet, vividly depicted the performance like this: rapid and soft notes mingled were just like big and small pearls dropping onto the jade plates.

[I] Afterwards, the pipa underwent improvement in playing techniques and structure. Players then changed from holding the pipa transversely to holding it vertically, and from using a pick to using the fingers to pluck the strings directly. In modern times, the volume and resonance has also been improved. The traditional music work "Spring Moonlight on the Flowers by the River", which has a history of over one hundred years, has brought harmony and a sense of beauty to untold numbers of people.

Erhu

[J] The erhu, also called "huqin", was introduced from the western region during the Tang Dynasty. During the Song Dynasty (960-1279), it was refined and improved, and new variations appeared. It was also an important instrument for playing the melody of Beijing Opera.

[K] When playing, the player usually stands the Erhu on his lap, and moves the bow across the vertical strings. The well-known music "Two Springs Reflect the Moon" was created by the blind folk artist Liu Yanjun, also named A Bing by the people. Though he could not see anything of the world, he played his Erhu using his heart and imagination. This melody conjures up a poetic night scene under the moonlight and expresses the composer's desolation and hope.

Flute

[L] The earliest flute was made from bone over 7,000 years ago. In the times since then, most flutes were made of bamboo, which allowed even common people to play it. By covering the holes and blowing through the side hole while moving the fingers flexibly between the six holes, a sound will be produced that is leisurely and mellifluous like sound from far away. This always reminds people of a pastoral picture of a farmer riding on a bull while playing a flute.

Ⅰ. Fast reading.

Direction: Each statement of the following contains information given in one of the paragraphs in the above passage. Identify the paragraph from which the information is derived. You may choose a paragraph more than once. Each paragraph is marked with a letter.

1. Beijing Opera, Chinese medicine and traditional Chinese painting are three cornerstones of Chinese culture.

2. The famous piece "Two Springs Reflect the Moon" conveys the composer's feelings of solitude and optimism.

3. There is a touching tale associated with the horse-headed fiddle, a musical instrument cherished deeply by the Mongolian people.

4. Throughout history, bamboo became the primary material for most flutes, enabling even common people to play this instrument.

5. During the Yuan Dynasty, qu, another form of literature influenced by music, gained widespread popularity.

6. Originating from the western region, huqin made its way into China during the Tang Dynasty.

7. In ancient times, ordinary people did not have the opportunity to experience music produced using chimes and bells.

8. Numerous renowned writers and poets composed verses and references about pipa in their literary works.

9. Chinese peasants displayed remarkable creativity by composing folk songs, which evolved independently with distinct regional characteristics.

10. Marco Polo's travels through Asia introduced the horse-headed fiddle to Europe, influencing European string music.

Ⅱ. Translate the following paragraph into English.

笛子是一种来自中国古代的乐器,也是中国乐器中最具代表性的吹奏乐器(wind instrument)之一。中国竹笛(the Chinese bamboo flute)是中国传统音乐中常用的乐器之一,也常在西洋交响乐团(the Western symphony orchestra)和现代音乐中得以运用。笛子在中国古人的观念中早已被赋予了"文化"的含义,有着不可替代的深远影响。诗人们过去常常以听到笛声后的感受作诗。在乐队中,笛子作为一种吹奏乐器有着举足轻重的地位,被称作"民乐之王"。

Passage 2

A Brief Overview of the Origins and Advancement of American Music

[1] American music is considered to be the most influential in the world. If you have often wondered why that is, it's important to note that it didn't happen by accident. You see, American music happens to be a huge melting pot, with influences from all parts of the world reflecting the diverse kinds of people who have settled in the United States over several centuries. This guide will attempt to give a simple overview of American music history so you can get a basic understanding of where it started to what it is now. Let's go.

The origins of American music

[2] Before Europeans arrived in North America, Native Americans had their own distinctive styles of music. The music of these early settlers was not well documented. Today, pow wow, which is practiced by many Native Americans, is among the few musical practices that endured through the years.

[3] The arrival of Europeans, particularly the British in the 16th Century, was a major turning point for the American music scene. They brought their music with them— including drinking songs, hymns, theater songs, and ballads— which they performed among their countrymen, as well as fused with the music of the Native Americans. People from France and Germany also brought their own music to different parts of America, with German settlers in Pennsylvania performing hymns in their native tongues and French music gaining a foothold in New Orleans.

[4] Not long after, the introduction of slavery also brought the African American musical influence. The Africans brought their "work" songs, which seemingly assisted with the arduous tasks they were burdened with, as well as spiritual songs. These two distinct sounds later influenced modern genres. Spiritualism, for example, preceded Christian music.

[5] Another sound that helped to shape American music was Appalachian folk styles. These included folk music created predominantly by both African Americans and Irish and Scottish people. The songs were often performed in combination (both black and white communities) and reflected way of life living in post-independent America. Appalachian folk music was the starting point for bluegrass and honky-tonk, which evolved into what is now known as Country music.

The fusing of sounds to form American pop music

[6] Now that we have an idea of where most of the sounds shaping modern American music

came from, let's look at how musicians used them over the years to create popular songs. The term "pop" literally means popular music. One of the defining factors of popular American music is that it tends to borrow from other genres. Various records show that the idea of popular music, which is music that resonated with a wide cross-section of people, began with minstrel shows in post-colonial America circa 1840s. These shows initially had a racist connotation — black-faced white performers imitating and exaggerating the sounds and styles of African American songs and dances. These shows had large audiences and grew in popularity in the northern parts of the country.

[7] During and after the Civil War period, African Americans also created their own minstrel shows for their black communities. One of the features of these black minstrel shows was a dance segment called a "cakewalk" where the couple with the most outstanding dance moves received a cake for their efforts. Later on, these cakewalk shows would evolve into a style of music called ragtime.

[8] In tandem with ballads and patriotic songs that had been passed down through the descendants of the Europeans, as well as the folk songs created by country folk, the American music scene slowly began to take shape. Before long, a number of artists were making a name for themselves across the US mainland. Tin Pan Alley, formed in the 1880s, became a hub where music creators of the day could get their songs sold as sheet music. "Pocket songsters" also assisted with the dissemination of the music being created, giving more ears to tunes that were created for particular groups and demographics.

[9] Music that had been confined to respective ethnic groups— minstrel shows for white and black, country songs for Southern audiences, etc. — could now be disseminated to the wider populace to be enjoyed by anyone, regardless of race or background.

[10] For example, "My Wild Irish Rose," an Irish ballad written in 1899, became popular among non-Irish people who would perform the song as well. Jazz and blues music, products of the African American community, also became popular with white Americans who not only listened to such songs but themselves started performing and creating works in these genres.

[11] The growth of the music industry during the latter part of the 19th Century and early 1900s was explosive with the coming of radio stations and TV, as well as the invention of the gramophone. The formation of ASCAP and a number of other music regulatory bodies provided a framework for songwriters to get paid for their works, which encouraged more and more Americans from all walks of life to embrace music as a way to make a living.

[12] But American music was not just simply about people writing songs; it was about being innovative, constantly trying to create a new sound. Songwriters and artists borrowed from and modified sounds and styles from other genres. Pretty soon, artists like Elvis Presley were performing songs that were deemed to have an African American sound while Ray Charles, a black singer with a Blues background, managed to land hits that had ballad ("Georgia on My Mind") and country music ("You Are My Sunshine") origins.

[13] In between, new sounds emerged while others phased out. For example, blues birthed a new sound called boogie-woogie, popular among African American communities. Sometime during the 1940s, boogie-woogie evolved into rock and roll, a sound that attracted the youth of the day and brought about the idea of a teen heartthrob (Frank Sinatra and Elvis, for example). Jazz had also taken on and was creating stars, especially among black performers.

[14] During the 1940s-1960s era, the identity of American music had well and truly been established, especially with the recording industry becoming more sophisticated. The creation of new instruments such as the electric guitar and synthesizer also helped with the definition of each new sound. There was the doo-wop sound, the bebop, soul, prog-rock, glam rock, and psychedelic rock. Rock stars emerged in the form of Jimi Hendrix, Lonnie Mack, Bob Dylan, and many others, albeit with different styles and different messages.

[15] At the same time, country-pop, which appealed mostly to mainly white audiences was being refined and became a mainstay in areas such as Nashville. To this day, Nashville remains a hub for country music and numerous country stars have honed their craft in that city.

[16] As time passed, American music had a growing influence on cultures from near and far. People from these cultures put their own interpretation on the sounds. The Beatles, for instance, came with their own brand of rock music in the 1960s, which in turn, helped to influence the next generation of pop.

[17] Other famous artists in the US such as Aretha Franklin and James Brown proved to be pioneers in their own rights as they also influenced pop music with their interpretation of soul/ blues and funk music respectively.

[18] Coming into the 1980s, rap/hip-hop was added to the mix of popular music. This type of music was derived from the act of introducing DJ music at predominantly African American parties. Rappers would not only hone their skills spitting lyrics over a beat, but they also popularized the idea of sampling other records. Hits by LL Cool J, Tupac Shakur, and Notorious B. I. G. have sampled riffs and phrases from genres as diverse as doo-wop to rock. Today, hip-hop has overtaken rock as the most popular genre among Americans. Also, sampling is practiced not just in hip-hop but in rhythm and blues, country, and pop tunes in general.

Other genres adding to the melting pot of American music

[19] The continuous influx of immigrants from all parts of the world has continued to diversify the sound of American music. Latin music, for example, which made its way from Mexico and Cuba have periodically churned out hits that crossed over from the Latin community into wider society. The most recent examples of this include "Despacito" by Luis Fonsi and "Havana" by Camilo Cabello.

[20] Gospel music, which evolved from the spiritual songs often sung by slaves, has also remained popular, especially among people who follow the Christian religion. Nowadays, however, gospel is more rooted in the soul/R&B sound, a trend made popular by Aretha

Franklin, among others.

[21] Not to be left out is classical music, which has its roots in Europe but has become ingrained in the American musical landscape. While classical music from famous composers was largely practiced by descendants of European immigrants who came in the 1700s, the genre would become "Americanized" with the setting up of the First New England School later on. Between the 19th and 20th Centuries, classical music would continue to be impacted, with musicians such as Leonard Bernstein and George Gershwin infusing jazz and spiritualism into their compositions. Later on, classical music became a big part of the Broadway scene as well as the movie industry (scores).

[22] American music has many more parts to it that could cover several blog posts and still only scratch the surface. Hopefully, this post will serve as a simple guide for those of you who might want to see how the music industry in the United States evolved from the early days to its current state.

I. Answer the following questions.

1. What types of music did Europeans bring with them when they arrived in North America?

2. What role did African Americans play in shaping American music, particularly during and after the Civil War period?

3. Where did hip-hop music originate from and what idea did rappers popularize?

4. How did classical music influence other genres in America, such as Broadway and the movie industry?

5. What is the significance of the continuous influx of immigrants in shaping American music, and how has it added to the country's musical diversity?

II. Translate the following paragraph into Chinese.

Music means different things to different people and sometimes even different things to the same person at different moments of his life. It might be poetic, philosophical, sensual, or mathematical, but in any case it must, in my view, have something to do with the soul of the human being. Hence it is metaphysical; but the means of expression is purely and exclusively physical: sound. I believe it is precisely this permanent coexistence of metaphysical message through physical means that is the strength of music. It is also the reason why when we try to describe music with words, all we can do is to articulate our reactions to it, and not grasp music itself.

Cross-cultural Perspectives

Read the following paragraph and write a summary of 200 words.

●●● The Man Who Journeyed to the Heart of Peking Opera ●●●

[1] The adage about Peking Opera still rings true: one minute of performance on stage requires 10 years of practice offstage. This sums up the rigorous training required for Peking Opera, the vivid, highly stylized ancient Chinese art form with a history of more than 200 years, which combines music, dance, drama, acrobatics and martial arts.

[2] For Nadim Diab, or Li Long as his Chinese name, a Lebanese who lives and works in Beijing, has taken this adage to heart as he takes part in a 100-day training program by professional Peking Opera actors and actresses.

[3] "Few people understand Peking Opera, though many have watched or heard about Peking Opera," Diab says.

[4] "Beauty and difficulty are two sides of the same coin in Peking Opera. Behind each peak you conquer in Peking Opera is an even taller mountain waiting to be tackled."

[5] "When people go to watch a Peking Opera show, they expect to witness a show like no other and they never walk away disappointed. Stellar performances are a guarantee in Peking Opera, but the behind-the-scenes workings are an untold story," says Diab.

[6] "The pain, the sacrifices, the long hours of daily practice and the constant pursuit to push one's physical and mental limits to the extreme. Every performer I met has poured their

blood, sweat and tears into this craft and makes a conscious decision every day to wake up and do it all over again."

[7] The 32-year-old Diab, who came to China in 2012 for his master's degree in global business journalism at Tsinghua University in Beijing, had his first encounter with Peking Opera a few years back when he watched a workshop online that Mu Yuandi gave in the United States in 2014. The Shanghai-based actor Mu specializes in the art of nandan (a male who plays a female role). This tradition was forged out of necessity. For much of its history in the old, feudal society, women were forbidden to perform Peking Opera.

[8] "He started from zero to perform as a Peking Opera actor, which was very difficult, such as leg stretching exercises," says Liu, 41, who, born and raised in the city of Jilin in Jilin province, was trained to become a Peking Opera actor as a child by his parents, both professional Peking Opera performers.

[9] "The sophisticated ancient art form is the essence of Chinese culture, which shows traditional Chinese values, such as loyalty, modesty and honesty. Even for professional performers, who spent years learning and practicing, the art form is much more than the primary appeal it appears to be, like brilliant costumes, the acrobatics and jaw-dropping skills."

[10] Peking Opera, also known as jingju in Chinese, was declared an Intangible Cultural Heritage of Humanity by UNESCO in 2010.

[11] In 1790, when four Hui Opera troupes visited Beijing as part of celebrations for the 80th birthday of the Emperor Qianlong (1711-99), they stayed in the south of the city. Hui opera, or huiju, is a form of Peking Opera from Anhui province. In about 1840, Peking Opera began to formally take shape, growing rapidly during the reign of Empress Dowager Cixi (1835-1908), a Chinese opera lover. After this, the art form went from strength to strength, with troupes being formed in Beijing, Tianjin and Shanghai.

[12] Peking Opera had its heyday with star performers popularizing the art form across the country as well as abroad. One of the best-known Peking Opera masters is Mei Lanfang, a nandan performer, who was the first actor to present Peking Opera outside China. He toured the US in 1930, visiting New York, Chicago and San Francisco. The tour lasted five weeks, rather than its originally scheduled two, due to the great acclaim he received.

[13] Zhang Huoding, one of the most famous contemporary Peking Opera performers, caused a sensation in 2015 by performing the famous Peking Opera pieces, *The Legend of the White Snake* and *The Jewelry Pouch*, in New York.

[14] In 2006, he got a role in award-winning composer Tan Dun's opera, *The First Emperor*, which, commissioned and staged at the Metropolitan Opera in New York, was directed by Chinese filmmaker Zhang Yimou and performed by Placido Domingo.

[15] "When the audiences reacted warmly to Peking Opera, I was impressed. I felt then that I should not give up the art form," recalls Liu, who moved to Beijing and joined in the China National Peking Opera Company in 2008.

[16] Yi Ling from the China National Peking Opera Company's foreign affairs office says that the company has been launching online programs to expand fan base not only in China but also abroad.

[17] "We are glad to see a revival of Peking Opera during the past few years, especially the young people who come to see our shows both in theaters and online," says Yi.

Case Study

Sun Run, a guzheng teacher from Beijing Language and Culture University, has taught nearly 100 foreign students across 50 countries on five continents how to play guzheng. She thinks it is still popular today with young people, both Chinese young and foreign young people. She says: "The foreign young people I met, they are very curious about Chinese guzheng or Chinese music. After they learned from me, they can play some music they love or the very popular, famous music from their country on guzheng. We have a saying that 'What belongs to the nation belongs to the world.' I hope people can establish the relationship through music and we can understand each other more."

Work collaboratively in groups to produce a 5-minute video illustrating your comprehension of the global appeal of traditional Chinese music, particularly the guzheng, and the cultural exchange it fosters.

6-2　Unit 6 译文及答案

Unit 7
Architecture

Unit Objectives

- To acquire vocabulary and expressions related to architecture in China and the West.
- To gain a general knowledge of the characteristics of architecture in China and the West.
- To express informed opinions and thoughtful analysis about architecture.
- To develop a sense of appreciation and confidence in Chinese architecture.

Read and Discuss

Read the following paragraph and discuss the following questions.

We will make sure the cultural sector prioritizes social benefit while also producing economic returns, deepen reform of the cultural management system, and improve economic policy for the cultural sector. We will implement a national cultural digitization strategy, improve the modern system of public cultural services, and launch new public-benefit cultural programs. We will improve the modern systems for cultural industries and markets and implement major cultural projects to spur the development of the sector. We will put more effort into protecting cultural artifacts and heritage, better protect and preserve historical and cultural heritage in the course of urban and rural development, and build and make good use of national cultural parks.

1. How well do you understand national cultural parks and their importance?

2. What are some examples of national cultural parks in China and what cultural heritage do they showcase?

3. How can national cultural parks contribute to the preservation and promotion of architectural heritage?

Section A

▼ Knowledge Focus

Ⅰ. **Fill in the blanks based on your understanding of the online video lectures.**

●●● *Ancient Chinese Architecture* ●●●

For over 3,000 years, Chinese architecture has flourished, showcasing a wide range of styles and structures. From 1) _____ imperial palaces to serene pagodas, each type of ancient Chinese architecture holds its own unique significance. Let's explore the key features and historical context of five 2) _____ architectural styles.

Imperial palaces were 3) _____ built to serve the extravagant lifestyles of the emperors, as well as to provide a centralized location for demonstrating imperial political control. The imperial palaces were built on a grand scale, 4) _____ no expense to display the majesty and dignity of the imperial power of the time. Each 5) _____ emperor contributed grandeur to the structures, and today, these palaces stand for all to enjoy. Each imperial palace is a 6) _____ to the history and glory of Chinese culture.

7-1
5 Types of Ancient Chinese Architecture—with Famous Examples
扫码观看视频

These glorious structures clearly demonstrate the creative 7)_____ and traditions of the Chinese people.

A prime example is the Forbidden City, located in Beijing. It stands as the largest ancient 8)_____ complex globally and is now home to the Palace Museum. Built between 1406 and 1420, the imperial palace is a complex 9)_____ 980 preserved ancient wood and stone buildings. Now, the Palace Museum houses and displays artwork, treasures, and 10)_____ from the Ming (1368-1644) and Qing (1644-1911) Dynasties.

Ⅱ. **Choose the best answer to each of the following questions.**

1. What is the main characteristic of traditional Chinese architecture?
A. Strict hierarchy rules.
B. Modern tall buildings.
C. Landscape gardens.
D. Bilateral asymmetry.

2. What concept does bilateral symmetry represent in traditional Chinese architecture?
A. Regional diversities.
B. Independent system.
C. Yin and Yang balance.
D. Technological development.

3. Why are traditional Chinese buildings usually single-story and small?
A. To reflect regional diversities.
B. To accommodate a large population.
C. To promote technological development.
D. To survive earthquakes and heavy winds.

4. Which ancient Chinese architectural structure is the largest and most complete complex of ancient wooden structures in the world?
A. Imperial Palaces.
B. Forbidden City.
C. Great Wall.
D. Big Wild Goose Pagoda.

5. Which animal is regarded as a symbol of power and strength in Chinese culture?
A. Horse
B. Phoenix.

C. Lion.

D. Elephant.

6. What is the purpose of the Temple of Heaven in Chinese architecture?

A. To pray to heaven for a good harvest.

B. To serve as a prime example of altars and temples.

C. To house monks who study Buddhist scriptures.

D. To honor the first emperor of China.

7. Which of the following is a characteristic feature of Victorian homes?

A. Flat roofs.

B. Minimalist design.

C. Sliding sash windows.

D. Symmetrical façade.

8. What contributed to the popularity of Cape Cod style during the early 20th century?

A. Introduction by European settlers.

B. Industrial revolution.

C. Influence of modernist architecture.

D. Great Depression and post-war housing boom.

9. In which city is the Empire State Building located?

A. Los Angeles.

B. Chicago.

C. San Francisco.

D. New York City.

10. Who is the Washington Monument dedicated to?

A. Abraham Lincoln.

B. George Washington.

C. Thomas Jefferson.

D. Theodore Roosevelt.

Ⅲ. Decide whether each of the following statements is true (T) or false (F).

1. Traditional Chinese buildings are primarily square-shaped with north-south orientations.

2. Traditional Chinese buildings are usually multilayered and used for bedrooms or studies.

Unit 7 Architecture

3. Timber was widely used in ancient Chinese architecture because it represents birth and life.

4. The main colors of the Forbidden City are red and green.

5. The Great Wall of China was originally made of stone.

6. The Big Wild Goose Pagoda is a seven-storied wooden structure.

7. The Empire State Building is located on Fourth Avenue in downtown Manhattan.

8. The Golden Gate Bridge connects San Francisco peninsula from its northern tip to Marin County.

9. The White House is the official residence and workplace of the President of the United States.

10. Mount Rushmore features sculptures of five presidents of the United States.

Language Focus

I. **Match the words and definitions.**

____align   ____conceive   ____decorative   ____extravagant
____hierarchy   ____magnitude   ____monument   ____resemble
                ____symmetry   ____testament

A. a thing that shows that something else exists or is true

B. the great size or importance of something; the degree to which something is large or important

C. to arrange something in the correct position, or to be in the correct position, in relation to something else, especially in a straight line

D. spending a lot more money or using a lot more of something than you can afford or than is necessary

E. a building, column, statue, etc. built to remind people of a famous person or event

F. to form an idea, a plan, etc. in your mind; to imagine something

G. to look like or be similar to another person or thing

H. (of an object or a building) decorated in a way that makes it attractive; intended to look attractive or pretty

I. a system, especially in a society or an organization, in which people are organized into different levels of importance from highest to lowest

J. the exact match in size and shape between two halves, parts or sides of something

II. There are 10 errors altogether in the following paragraph(s). The errors are: missing words, unnecessary words and wrong words. Please correct them as follows: for a missing word, mark its position with the symbol "∧" and write it; for an unnecessary word, cross it out with the symbol "\"; for a wrong word, underline it and write the correct word.

Throughout ancient Chinese history, the hierarchy had been strict followed and highly valued by Confucianism. In the architecture field, structure, pattern, color, decoration, and scale all had explicit regulation according to one's social status. For instance, except for unique buildings as religious pagodas, no one's house could be taller or more prominent then the emperor's Imperial Palaces; in some dynasties, civilians were not allowed use specific auspicious patterns like the Dragon or Phoenix, or some noble colors like Cinnabar Red and Bright Yellow. According to Yin Yang and Five Elements Theory, balance is an essential and highly valued concept. Hence, bilateral symmetry, which believed to be a great representation of	1. _____ 2. _____ 3. _____ 4. _____ 5. _____ 6. _____ 7. _____ 8. _____

the balance of Yin and Yang, have been strictly used in traditional Chinese buildings, except for Landscape Gardens. Moreover, in a bilateral symmetrical ancient building complex, the grand and most important ones are always located in the central line.

9. _____

10. _____

▼ Critical Thinking

Discuss the following questions in small groups and share your ideas in class.

1. What cultural influences have shaped the distinctive characteristics of Chinese and American architecture?

2. How do Chinese architecture and American architecture differ in the use of materials and construction techniques?

3. What are the environmental sustainability practices in Chinese and American architecture, and how effective are they?

4. How might cultural exchange and globalization impact the future development of Chinese and American architectural styles?

5. What are the key factors that contribute to the aesthetic appeal of Chinese and American architecture?

6. How do personal biases and cultural backgrounds influence our perception and understanding of Chinese and American architecture?

▼ Case Study

The creation of the Walt Disney World Resort remains one of the most impressive features of engineering, construction and artistry ever attempted. The architectural firm you work for has been entrusted with the task of constructing a Disney theme park in Wuhan. There are differing opinions within the team regarding whether to replicate the American Disney parks or to infuse the design with Chinese elements.

As a professional architect, you are supposed to work out a design plan and provide the reasoning behind it.

Section B

Passage 1

10 Things We Can Learn from Chinese Architecture

[1] Chinese architecture can be broadly distinguished into two parts: Traditional and modern. While ancient traditional Chinese architecture has a distinct style and defining characteristics, modern Chinese architecture is still finding its rhythm.

[2] Some distinct features of traditional Chinese architecture are symmetry, hierarchy in the built environment, the cosmological influence of Feng Shui, horizontal expansion rather than vertical, gardens, courtyards, and a distinct construction system. These features play a crucial role in shaping the overall aesthetics and functionality of traditional Chinese architecture.

1. Symmetry

[3] Symmetry has been one of the oldest and most influential ordering principles in architecture and it helps unify various elements together. Symmetry in architecture is widely used because unlike other applications, it is not only visually pleasing to look at, but we can also experience symmetry by moving through it.

[4] It is closely linked with the repetition of mass and void to dictate movement and experience which results in axial relationships.

2. Chinese gardens

[5] Chinese gardens are a distinctly evolved landscape style that is based on three kinds of conceptions: aspire, immoral, and natural. Each of these is found in different classes of society: royalty, temples, and scholars respectively. Looking beyond the class division, it becomes evident how the aspects of the theories of philosophy, politics, virtue, and aesthetics are reflected in these gardens.

[6] The balance of the relation of all the elements: water, architecture, vegetation, and rocks, is gracefully integrated into these gardens to become a paradise for humans amongst nature. In a modern world, these hold the potential to become powerful places of relief from the claustrophobic growing urban density in the cities. Placed intelligently, these could ironically become equalizers across different classes of society and be a peaceful and calming place for all.

3. Indigenous construction system

[7] Traditional Chinese architecture was built using a wooden frame structure. Wood is easily available in this region and can easily adapt to varying climates and is suitable in earthquake-prone regions such as this.

[8] The dry timber construction was erected through structural joineries and dowelling alone. Instead of nails and glue, interlocking elements like the Dougong are used. This would prevent buckling and torsion under high compression, and allow for the building to absorb shock vibrations from earthquakes.

4. Siheyuan

[9] Siheyuan is a courtyard typically found in traditional Chinese dwellings. The degree of enclosure defines the level of intimacy of the open. While it is a concept popularly used in housing typology, variants of it can be seen across all kinds of buildings and complexes.

[10] Courtyards are beneficial for more than just spatial reasons, they are used to regulate temperature and ventilate the building. These courtyards are traditionally open and face towards the south to allow maximum exposure to the sun while blocking the cold northern winds. Frequently, the scale of the courtyard is so small that it just serves as a light shaft that serves to collect and harvest rainwater from the sloping rooftops. Moreover, they also serve as vents to allow hot air to rise up and out, and cool air to enter the building.

5. Feng Shui

[11] Feng Shui is an ancient Chinese concept of geomancy derived from Chinese cosmology, Confucianism and Taoism. These dictate the organizational principles and construction layouts from simple dwellings to imperial structures.

[12] It is believed that embodiments of evil and their energy travel in straight lines. Hence, a screen wall usually faces the main entrance of the house. Moreover, talismans, images of gods, and Fu Lu Shou are displayed at the entrance to ward off evil spirits. Certain colors, numbers, and cardinal orientations are believed to reflect a type of immanence.

[13] The larger orientation of the building is along its north-south axis with its back facing an elevated landscape to ensure that water collects in the front. Moreover, the back of the structure is usually facing north with minimal or no openings to protect the inhabitants from the harsh northern winter winds.

[14] Bodies of water like pools, ponds, and wells, are typically built into the structure as a way to indicate the self-sustenance of the household. Moreover, a body of water is said to nourish the soul through its calming effect and hence is a celebrated element in Chinese architecture.

6. Urban Planning

[15] Chinese political power as well as their reflection of the built communities was articulated by the boundary defining the outer and inner. Cities were built by creating a progression of gated communities that allowed the owner of the household of the ruler to feel safe inside.

[16] As one would enter the gate, the buildings on the periphery would be public in nature and as one moved towards the inside, it became increasingly private and secure. The movement from one building to another was through intervening courtyards and hence limited access to the core of the complex. One such example is the emperor's palace which due to this reason was named the "Forbidden City".

[17] Recently, however, contemporary Chinese architecture is moving on; it is now referring inwards to itself rather than outside to others. This coming-of-age phase in architecture brought about many iconic buildings that are an example of the perfect blend of traditional and contemporary architecture.

7. Traditional elements in contemporary architecture

[18] After the late 1970s when the Chinese economic reform initiated a new period in China, where Chinese architects began reconsidering the international architectural trends led by the West. A particularly revolutionary project built by an American Chinese architect I. M. Pei was the Fragrant Hill Hotel in Beijing. He created an influential masterpiece by combining his knowledge of the modern styles from the west and his deep-rooted Chinese culture.

[19] Following the tendency of horizontality, the hotel is a low-slung building set in a natural landscape. It reflected the vernacular language of white walls and grey tiles with a central atrium. To top it off he also created a Chinese garden maze using multiple vanishing points leading to a delightful surprise at every turn.

[20] While traditional Chinese architecture is iconic and well defined in its own way. Many aspects of it need change to accommodate the needs of the people and to keep up with current times.

8. Mixed-use buildings

[21] Traditional Chinese architecture was strictly differentiated typology based on its programmatic functions. However, learning from the western influence, an increasing number of buildings and complexes have adopted a mixed-use approach. The Water Cube is one such example that was built to host the 2008 Summer Olympics and Paralympics but is now a place to shop, eat, and socialize.

9. Open floor plan

[22] Modern Chinese architecture takes on a sleek and futuristic appearance with buildings that are more streamlined and open concept rather than the traditional modular pavilion concept approach. This allows for a free flow of form and large open spaces that make their mark in the public sphere of China which was earlier posing to be a significant issue. The National Grand Theater of China is one such example of Chinese modern architecture.

10. Verticality

[23] While traditional Chinese architecture was largely horizontal and low-rise, the massive population growth has forced the country to build upward and not outward, creating iconic skylines.

I. Answer the following questions.

1. What are some distinct features of traditional Chinese architecture?

2. Why was wood the primary construction material in traditional Chinese architecture?

3. How do courtyards contribute to sustainable practices in traditional Chinese architecture?

4. What is Feng Shui, and how does it influence Chinese architecture?

5. What is the significance of mixed-use buildings in modern Chinese architecture?

II. Translate the following paragraph into English.

赵州桥建于隋朝,公元605年左右,长50.82米,宽9.6米,跨度37.37米。天才建筑师李春设计并监督了桥的建设。赵州桥结构新颖、造型优美。桥有一个大拱,在大拱的两端有两个小拱,帮助排泄洪水、减轻桥梁重量并节省石材。建成以来,该桥经受了多次洪水和地震,但其主体结构仍然完好无损,至今仍在使用。赵州桥是世界桥梁建筑史上的一次创举,是中国古代文明史上的一项杰出成就。类似设计的桥梁直到14世纪才在欧洲出现,比赵州桥晚了700多年。

Passage 2

France's Beloved Cathedral Only Minutes Away from Complete Destruction

[A] Notre Dame Cathedral in the heart of Paris was within "15 to 30 minutes" of complete destruction as firefighters battled to stop flames reaching its bell towers on Monday evening, French authorities have revealed. A greater disaster was averted by members of the Paris fire brigade, who risked their lives to remain inside the burning monument to create a wall of water between the raging fire and the two towers on the west of the building.

[B] The revelation of how close France came to losing its most famous cathedral emerged as police investigators questioned workers involved in the restoration of the monument to try to establish the cause of the devastating blaze. Paris prosecutor Remy Heitz said that an initial fire alert was sounded at 6:20 pm on Monday evening but no fire was found. The second alert was sounded at 6:43 pm, and the blaze was discovered on the roof.

[C] More than €650 million was raised in a few hours on Tuesday as French business leaders and global corporations announced they would donate to a restoration campaign launched by the president, Emmanuel Macron. But as the emergency services picked through the burnt debris, a row was resurfacing over accusations that the beloved cathedral, immortalized in Victor Hugo's novel, was already crumbling before the fire.

[D] The cathedral is owned by the French state and has been at the centre of a years-long dispute over who should finance restoration work of the collapsing staircases, crumbling statues and cracked walls. Jean-Michel Leniaud, the president of the scientific council at the National Heritage Institute, said: "What happened was bound to happen. The lack of adequate maintenance and daily attention to such a majestic building is the cause of this catastrophe." After the blaze was declared completely extinguished, 15 hours after it started, the junior interior minister, Laurent Nunez, said the structure had been saved but remained vulnerable. He praised the actions of the firefighters but admitted the fate of the cathedral had been uncertain. "They saved the main structure, but it all came down to 15-30 minutes," Nunez said.

[E] In a surprise televised address on Tuesday evening, Macron said he wanted to see the cathedral rebuilt within five years. "The fire at Notre Dame reminds us that we will always have challenges to overcome," Macron said. "Notre Dame is our history, our literature, the centre of our life. It is the standard by which we measure our distances. It's so many books, so many paintings. It's the cathedral of every French person, even those who have never visited it. This history is ours and so we will rebuild Notre Dame. It is what the French people expect; it is what our history deserves. It is our deep destiny. We will rebuild Notre Dame so it is even more beautiful than before. I want it done in the next five years. We can do it. After the time of testing comes a time of reflection and then of action."

[F] The fire, which had started at the base of the 93-metre spire (尖塔) at about 6:40 p.m. on Monday, spread through the cathedral's roof, made up of hundreds of oak beams, some dating back to the 13th century. These beams, known as la forêt (the forest) because of their density, formed the cross-shaped roof that ran the length of the central part of the cathedral. As hundreds of tourists and Parisians stood and watched the flames leaping from the roof, there was shock and tears as the cathedral spire caught fire, burned and then collapsed into itself.

[G] A collection of dramatic videos and photos quickly spread across social media, showing the horrifying destruction, and attracting emotional responses from people all over the world. Indeed, within minutes the fire occupied headlines of every major global newspaper and television network. This is not surprising given Notre Dame Cathedral, meaning "Our Lady", is one of the most recognized symbols of the city of Paris attracting millions of tourists every year.

[H] While the world looked on, the 500 firefighters at the scene then battled to prevent the flames from reaching the two main towers, where the cathedral bells hang. If the wooden frame of the towers had caught fire, it could have sent the bells— the largest of which, the Emmanuel Bell, weighs 13 tons— crashing down, potentially causing the collapse of both towers. Police and fire services will spend the next 48 hours assessing the "security and safety" of the 850-year-old structure. Nunez said: "We have identified vulnerabilities throughout the structure, all of which still need securing." As a result, residents of five buildings around the northern side of the cathedral were being temporarily evacuated, he added. Architects have identified three main holes in the structure, in the locations of the spire, the main hall and the upper rooms to the north of the central aisle. Most of the wooden roof beams have been burned, and parts of the concrete holding up the roof have collapsed.

[I] The interior minister, Christophe Castaner, visited the cathedral on Tuesday afternoon to see the extent of the devastation. Ash covered the marble diamond-patterned floor and floated in large pools of grey water from the fire hoses. Behind a heap of blackened oak beams that lay piled up where they had fallen, daylight from vast holes in the cathedral roof lit a golden cross over a statue by Nicolas Coustou, which appeared to have escaped damage. Preliminary inspections also suggested the three ornate (装饰华丽的) stained glass "rose" windows appeared to have survived the fire, officials said. However, fire officers have said a complete inventory of the damage will not be possible until the cathedral structure has been deemed safe.

[J] The culture minister, Franck Riester, said religious relics saved from the cathedral were being securely held at the Hôtel de Ville, and works of art that sustained smoke damage were being taken to the Louvre, the world's largest art museum, where they would be dried out, repaired and stored. Sixteen copper statues that decorated the spire had been removed for restoration only a few days before the fire. Relics at the top of the spire are believed lost as the spire was destroyed. As well as damage from the heat, which firefighters said reached more than

800 ℃, experts also need to assess damage from the vast quantities of water firefighters poured into the cathedral. One casualty of this was The Great Organ constructed in the 1730s, which was said to have escaped the flames but been significantly damaged by water.

[K] French political commentators noted the devastating fire had succeeded where Macron had failed in uniting the country. But criticism over the original state of the building is likely to intensify over coming days. Leniaud told *La Croix* newspaper: "This is not about looking for people to blame. The responsibility is collective because this is the most loved monument in the country." Alexandre Gady, an art historian, agreed. "We've been saying for years that the budget for maintaining historic monuments is too low," Gady said. The Paris prosecutor's office has opened an inquiry into "involuntary destruction by fire", indicating they believe the cause of the blaze was accidental rather than criminal.

Ⅰ. Fast reading.

Direction: Each statement of the following contains information given in one of the paragraphs in the above passage. Identify the paragraph from which the information is derived. You may choose a paragraph more than once. Each paragraph is marked with a letter.

1. The total amount of damage to Notre Dame Cathedral can be assessed only when its structure is considered safe.

2. Once again people began to argue whether Notre Dame Cathedral was going to collapse even without the fire.

3. The Notre Dame Cathedral catastrophe was said to have helped unite the French nation.

4. The roof of Notre Dame Cathedral was built with large numbers of densely laid-out wood beams.

5. Renovation workers of Notre Dame Cathedral were questioned to find out the cause of the accident.

6. Had the bell towers' wooden frames burned down, the heavy bells would have crashed down.

7. The timely action of the firefighters prevented the fire from reaching the Cathedral's bell towers.

8. Apart from the fire, the water used to extinguish it also caused a lot of damage to Notre Dame Cathedral.

9. There has been argument over the years as to who should pay for the restoration of Notre Dame Cathedral.

10. News of the Notre Dame Cathedral catastrophe instantly caught media attention throughout the world.

Ⅱ. **Translate the following paragraph into Chinese.**

When it comes to recognizable skylines, New York City's tops the list. The Big Apple is known for its many impressive architectural firsts. Though Chicago may have invented the skyscraper, New York made it famous, and then took it to its extreme with the advent of the super-tall. These pencil-thin towers are new points of interest in the built landscape. But they are also highly visible markers of exorbitant wealth, the power of real estate, and architectural innovation.

Cross-cultural Perspectives

Read the following paragraph and write a report of 200 words to illustrate your interpretation.

••• Why Don't We Teach Chinese Architecture in the United States? •••

[1] How many U.S. architecture professors know that there is a Chinese treatise equivalent to Vitruvius' *Ten Books on Architecture*? Very few, I suspect. I taught architectural history for more than 20 years before I discovered the marvelous *Yingzao Fashi*, a Song Dynasty book by a prominent court official who, as far as we know, was not an architect or builder. In fact, prior to the Ming Dynasty, no prominent temple, palace, or shrine in China was designed by an architect because the concept of a single mastermind in charge of a building project was foreign to the East Asian way of designing environments of any kind.

[2] Though architectural history courses and texts now feature prehistoric, native, and non-Western architecture, as a result, time spent on the rich, longstanding tradition of East Asian building arts is scant in undergraduate curricula. As our society reevaluates its reliance on so

many white, Western, and elitist assumptions about culture, it is no longer acceptable to ignore one of the most important artistic contributions of the world's largest nation, and many surrounding countries that followed its lead in timber building for centuries. Nor is it beneficial to students who must adapt historic buildings for modern uses to be ignorant of beautiful, earthquake-proof structures that have stood through every kind of weather event with only minor maintenance—buildings constructed without nails, bricks, or glass windows.

[3] True, it is daunting for Western architects to gain any significant knowledge of the vast corpus of material that Chinese scholars have unearthed. As with much of their culture, the Chinese have been protective of their ancient artistic practices and have generally followed Western modern methods of building for most of the last century. Still, there are several recent publications in English that allow any curious architect or landscape architect to appreciate the magnificent achievements of the period between 1000 AD and 1500 AD, which many scholars believe was the golden age of building throughout what we now know as China. Only a rudimentary knowledge of Asian history is a prerequisite.

[4] One of the fascinating aspects of early Chinese building is its reliance on rammed earth platforms and hollowed-out spaces dug out of the earth for shelter. Only after timber harvesting proved feasible did the earliest builders develop their unique methods of joining wooden logs and fashioning "bracket sets" to support overhanging roofs. Fu Xinian, the greatest historian of Chinese buildings, has published research that literally excavates the history of his country's architecture from caves, mountainous shrines, and long-lost cities. Comparing archaeological evidence to extant structures, he documents a building tradition that matured rapidly and remained unchanged for more than a thousand years.

[5] Nancy Steinhardt, for decades the only American scholar with widespread publications on the subject, has a new book that provides a good summary of all the research undertaken by China's corps of architect-archaeologists over the past 40 years. Using her guide, architects can dip into the specialist literature that provides a deeper look into a fascinating building tradition, one that is a continuum, not a culture obsessed with novelty and passing fashions.

[6] By the year 1103, when Li Je created the official treatise on imperial buildings for the Song rulers, a complete proportional, structural, and constructional system for making buildings of any size and type was fully understood by carpenters and other craftsmen throughout the provinces, with minor variations from north to south. Li was simply recording the current wisdom (as was Vitruvius). The system is close enough to Greek classical buildings to invite direct comparison, something only one architect attempted from the 1920s until the 1950s. Liang Sicheng, a student of Paul Cret's at the University of Pennsylvania, spent his life measuring great monuments with his wife, Lin Whei-yin, created the amazing *Pictorial History of Chinese Architecture*, published in the West only in 1980. Like Francis D. K. Ching's famous *Architectural Graphics*, it tells its story primarily with annotated drawings. With notes in both Chinese and English, Liang created a masterpiece of erudition that could easily be used to teach Western students the rudiments of the Dou Gong bracket system. Today, on the internet, one can see Chinese architecture teachers making models of bracket sets to demonstrate the intricate, but ultimately simple, means by which cantilevered eaves were balanced on slender, round columns. There is also a demonstration of seismic forces on shaking a small timber building.

[7] The point here is not to downplay the challenges that Western architects face when trying to understand a tradition so opaque to many who were trained to revere Corbusier and Wright. It is simply to indicate the wealth of material now available to those who are curious about Chinese architecture and to suggest that educators take a good look at what they are missing. I know I was embarrassed to recognize my ignorance. I was lucky enough to have one or two Chinese students who challenged me during the last decade, and I am grateful for their tutelage.

[8] One student was interested in preserving Beijing's distinctive courtyard houses, the siheyuan, and hutongs, that were rapidly being destroyed by officials before and following the Olympics. He was concerned that the central government did not have the tools used by European and American planners to control development in historic urban quarters. Following a year of research, he was able to assess the crisis and return home with some new ideas for how to stem the tide of destruction that has besieged the Imperial City for decades. So it is not just Westerners who need to understand the richness of Chinese building, but also the officials who now manage historic resources in a rapidly developing nation.

[9] Though I have never visited Beijing or Shanghai, I long to see the intricate and surprising buildings I have studied in these superb books and videos. The buildings and gardens on my bucket list expanded recently to include at least 50 sites in China, a few in Korea, and many in Japan. Several U.S. universities, including USC, Kean University, NYU, and Yale, have Chinese or Asian campuses. More will follow, and all should emphasize the study of Chinese architecture. The world needs lessons from builders who used forest resources and native clay to make some of the most remarkable environments on earth.

▼ Case Study

What makes a building outstanding and emblematic of a city or even a nation is not easy. Many buildings are famous for their beauty, while others are celebrated for their inventiveness or historical significance. There are similarities and differences between Eastern and Western architecture in terms of style, history, materials, function, and influence. For example, the Forbidden City in China and Buckingham Palace in the UK both represent their respective countries and have influenced modern architectural design.

In terms of architectural style, the Forbidden City and Buckingham Palace reflect the cultural differences between the East and the West. The Chinese traditional style emphasizes "additive beauty", paying attention to the flow lines and artistic appeal of beams, columns, and roofs. The Forbidden City's roof design allows for rainwater drainage and sunlight while also showcasing its aesthetic appeal. On the other hand, Buckingham Palace follows a classical Greek aesthetic and emphasizes "form equals beauty". Both buildings are influenced by their respective cultures and focus on practicality.

Both the Forbidden City and Buckingham Palace have long histories. Buckingham Palace's site has been associated with royalty since the Middle Ages, with various owners and transfers of ownership over the centuries. Similarly, the construction of the Beijing Forbidden City began in 1406 during the Ming Dynasty and was completed in 1420, serving as the imperial palace for 24 emperors until the end of the Qing Dynasty in 1911.

The choice of building materials also differs between Eastern and Western architecture. In ancient times, Chinese architects primarily used wood, while Western architects favored masonry. The Forbidden City is predominantly made of wood, using 15 types of precious and corrosion-resistant timber. Buckingham Palace, on the other hand, features Bath limestone as its façade ornament material. The choice of materials contributes to the unique appearances of these buildings.

Both the Forbidden City and Buckingham Palace continue to serve important functions today. Buckingham Palace is the official residence of British monarchs and also houses administrative offices. It hosts official events, state visits, and investitures. The Forbidden City, a UNESCO World Heritage site, is open to tourists and showcases the pinnacle of classical architecture in China and East Asia. It has been a significant influence on Chinese architecture and a source of inspiration for many works of art.

The significance and influence of the Forbidden City and Buckingham Palace are considerable. Their architectural designs serve as models for modern architects. The

Forbidden City's spatial arrangement and artistic effects create an anticipation and appreciation for the art within. Ancient buildings like these bridge the past and present, providing a profound ambiance and beauty that continue to inspire.

Work collaboratively in groups to produce a 5-minute video illustrating your comprehension of the architectural styles that exemplify the cultural disparities between Eastern and Western architecture.

7-2　Unit 7 译文及答案

Unit 8
Medicine and Healthcare

Unit Objectives

· To acquire vocabulary and expressions related to medicine and healthcare in China and the West.
· To gain a general knowledge of the characteristics of architecture in China and the West.
· To express informed opinions and thoughtful analysis about medicine and healthcare.
· To develop a sense of building a community with a shared future for humanity.

Read and Discuss

Read the following paragraph and discuss the following questions.

We deeply implement the development ideology centered around the people, continuously exerting efforts in providing comprehensive support for the young, ensuring access to education, securing fair wages, offering medical care, providing elderly care, ensuring adequate housing, and offering assistance to the disadvantaged. The quality of life for the people is being comprehensively improved. The average life expectancy has increased to 78.2 years. The per capital disposable income for residents has risen from 16,500 yuan to 35,100 yuan. We have established the world's largest education system, social security system, and healthcare system. The level of education has achieved a historic leap, with basic pension insurance covering 1.04 billion people and the participation rate in basic medical insurance remaining stable at 95 percent.

1. How does the comprehensive support and development ideology of the people contribute to the overall well-being and quality of life for the population?

___

2. What are the key factors and strategies that have led to the significant increase in life expectancy and per capita disposable income?

___

3. What challenges might be associated with managing the establishment of the world's largest education, social security, and healthcare systems?

___

Section A

▼ Knowledge Focus

Ⅰ. **Fill in the blanks based on your understanding of the online video lectures.**

••• The Medical Technology Industry •••

The United States remains the largest medical device market in the world. The medical technology industry (commonly referred to as medical devices) consists of articles, instruments, 1) _____, or machines that are used in the prevention, diagnosis or treatment of illness or disease, or for detecting, measuring, restoring, correcting, or modifying the structure or function of the body for some health purpose. Typically, the purpose of a medical device is not achieved by pharmacological, 2) _____.

8-1
The Medical
Technology Industry
扫码观看视频

One of the components fueling the growth includes electro-medical equipment, which includes a variety of powered devices such as pacemakers, patient-monitoring systems, MRI machines, diagnostic imaging equipment (including informatics equipment) and ultrasonic scanning devices. Biotech companies are 3)_____ on an aging population, increasing incidence of chronic and lifestyle diseases and increasing adoption of innovative technology.

U. S. medical device companies are highly regarded globally for their innovative and high technology products. R&D spending continues to represent a high percentage of medical device industry 4)_____, averaging 7 percent of revenue. Compared to several other industries including automotive, defense, and telecommunications, the medical device industry invests a higher percentage of yearly revenues into product innovation, reflecting the 5)_____ nature of the industry and constant 6)_____ and improvement of existing technologies.

The medical device industry relies on several industries where the United States holds a competitive advantage, including microelectronics, 7)_____, instrumentation, biotechnology, and software development. 8)_____ have led to recent advances including neuro-stimulators, stent technologies, biomarkers, robotic assistance, and implantable electronic devices. Since innovation 9)_____ the medical device sector's ongoing quest for better ways to treat and diagnose medical conditions, when 10)_____ increasing and aging populations globally, the medical device sector should continue growing at a positive rate in the future.

Ⅱ. Choose the best answer to each of the following questions.

1. What philosophical concept is TCM based on?

   A. The human body is a small universe with interconnected systems.

   B. The human body is made up of separate and unrelated parts.

   C. The human mind is more important than the physical body.

   D. The physical body is more important than the mind.

2. Which method of diagnosis in TCM involves listening to the sound of the patients and smelling the odor of excreta released by the human body?

   A. Observation.

   B. Auscultation and olfaction.

   C. Interrogation.

   D. Pulse feeling and palpation.

3. What is the main difference between Traditional Chinese Medicine and Western medicine?

   A. Traditional Chinese Medicine promotes overall wellness, while Western medicine focuses on treating symptoms.

   B. Traditional Chinese Medicine sees results sooner, while Western medicine requires long-term persistence.

C. Traditional Chinese Medicine ignores the mind, spirit, and emotions, while Western medicine treats the whole person.

D. Traditional Chinese Medicine only uses herbal medicine, while Western medicine uses a variety of treatments.

4. What is the purpose of acupuncture in Traditional Chinese Medicine?
A. To increase the amount of yin in the body.
B. To influence the flow of blood in the body.
C. To influence the flow of qi in the body.
D. To strengthen the muscles in the body.

5. What is an Internet hospital?
A. A physical hospital that is located on the internet.
B. A hospital where patients are mainly treated with online consultations.
C. A hospital that specializes in treating internet-related health issues.
D. A platform for the delivery of remote medical services via internet technologies.

6. Why are patents important in pharmaceutical innovation?
A. They encourage competition.
B. They protect intellectual property.
C. They reduce the cost of drug development.
D. They ensure global distribution of drugs.

7. What are medical devices primarily used for?
A. Administering medication.
B. Boosting immune system.
C. Regulating metabolism.
D. Restoring body function.

8. What is the main reason for the growth of the medical device industry?
A. Collaboration with automotive companies.
B. Increasing adoption of innovative technology.
C. Reduction in chronic and lifestyle diseases.
D. Declining R&D spending.

9. How is the priority of care determined in the emergency room?
A. Based on the severity of the condition.
B. Based on the patient's blood type.

C. Based on the availability of medical equipment.

D. Based on the patient's medical history.

10. What can be done if you believe you've been overcharged for medical services?

A. Pay the bill without question.

B. Threaten legal action.

C. Negotiate a lower bill.

D. Ignore the bill and hope it goes away.

Ⅲ. Decide whether each of the following statements is true (T) or false (F).

1. Bian Que, an early physician, is traditionally credited with the founding of the four methods of diagnosis in Chinese medicine.

2. Moxibustion is the application of cold to specific points or areas on the body in TCM.

3. Fangcang hospitals are public places, such as conference centers and stadiums, that were converted into shelters for patients infected with COVID-19.

4. Medical personnel in China have not received any recognition or support for their efforts in fighting the epidemic.

5. 5G-enabled robots have been installed at hospitals to offer various automated medical services, but they do not reduce cross-infection.

6. Advancements in western medicine have not contributed to the quality of life and longevity.

7. Economic challenges have hindered the commitment of U. S. pharmaceutical companies to research and development of new medicines and treatments.

8. Ambulance rides are expensive due to a variety of factors such as labor, training, readiness, and equipment.

9. The cost of an ambulance ride only depends on the miles being driven.

10. Patients should not provide any information about their medical condition once they are in an emergency room.

Unit 8 Medicine and Healthcare

▼ Language Focus

Ⅰ. Match the words and definitions.

___apparatus　　___coverage　　___eligibility　　___expenditure
___immunological　　___monopoly　　___pharmaceutical　　___revenue
　　　　　___subsidize　　___supremacy

A. to give money to sb. or an organization to help pay for something

B. connected with making and selling drugs and medicines

C. a position in which you have more power, authority or status than anyone

D. the act of spending or using money; an amount of money spent

E. the range or quality of information that is included in a book or course of study, on television, etc.

F. the quality or state of being qualified or suitable for a particular purpose or status, often based on meeting certain criteria or requirements

G. the complete control of trade in particular goods or the supply of a particular service; a type of goods or a service that is controlled in this way

H. the tools or other pieces of equipment that are needed for a particular activity or task

I. pertaining to the immune system and its functions, including the body's ability to defend itself against diseases and foreign substances

J. the money that a government receives from taxes or that an organization, etc. receives from its business

Ⅱ. There are 10 errors altogether in the following paragraph(s). The errors are: missing words, unnecessary words and wrong words. Please correct them as follows: for a missing word, mark its position with the symbol "∧" and write it; for an unnecessary word, cross it out with the symbol "\"; for a wrong word, underline it and write the correct word.

What is Traditional Chinese Medicine (TCM)? It is a completely system of medicine that has developed over thousands of years.	1. _____

It is based on the philosophical concept which the human body is a small universe for a set of interconnected systems, that those systems usually work in balance to maintaining the healthy human body. This ancient holistic medical system which understands that the body, mind, spiritual and emotions must all be interconnected to restore balance in one's life.

The doctrines of Traditional Chinese Medicine are root in books such as *Yellow Emperor's Inner Canon* and *Treatise on Febrile and Miscellaneous Diseases*, as well in cosmological notion such as yin and yang and the five elements theory.

2. _____
3. _____
4. _____
5. _____
6. _____
7. _____

8. _____

9. _____
10. _____

▼ Critical Thinking

Discuss the following questions in small groups and share your ideas in class.

1. What are the main differences in healthcare systems between China and the United States?

2. How do the American healthcare policies affect the global landscape of healthcare including China?

3. How do cultural differences impact healthcare practices in China and the United States?

4. What are some possible reasons for the differences in healthcare systems between China and the United States?

5. How has technology impacted healthcare practices in both China and the United States?

6. How can individuals take an active role in managing their own health in China and the United States?

Case Study

You were studying at Duke University in Spring of 2021 in USA. Wearing masks was mandatory at campus in China. However, you found that most American students didn't wear masks.

Please write a report on this phenomenon.

Section B

Passage 1

An Overview of the Chinese Healthcare System

[1] The healthcare security system is an important institutional arrangement for reducing people's medical burden, improving people's well-being, and therefore maintaining social harmony and stability in China. The purpose of establishing a national medical security system is to relieve all people of their worries concerning illness and health care.

[2] The national medical security system in China is a multilevel system, with the basic medical insurance (BMI) as the pillar and medical aid as the backup, and commercial health insurance, charitable donations, and medical mutual aid activities as supplementary services.

[3] The BMI system serves two groups of people: employees and residents. Employees are enrolled in the employee basic medical insurance (EBMI) program, and non-working residents are enrolled in the residents basic medical insurance (RBMI) program. After being established in 2018, the National Healthcare Security Administration (NHSA) has continued to improve the national medical insurance system so that RBMI can be better integrated. As of September 2020, more than 1.35 billion people (over 95% of China's population) are covered by one of the BMI programs, making it the world's largest healthcare security network. Among those covered,

337 million are covered by the EBMI, and 1.014 billion people are covered by the RBMI. The medical insurance fund is sustainable and growing. In 2019, the revenue of the national basic medical insurance fund (including maternity insurance) was CNY ￥2.44 trillion, and the expenditure was CNY ￥2.09 trillion.

[4] Medical aid ensures all citizens have fair access to basic medical services by supporting the section of the low-income populace to participate in the BMI by subsidizing the medical expenses that they cannot afford. Since 2018, medical aid has benefited 480 million low-income citizens, helped reduce their medical burden by approximately CNY ￥330 billion, implemented targeted poverty reduction measures for 10 million people in need who were impoverished due to illnesses, and ensured their basic medical security. Various social forces in the market also actively participate in supplementing the medical security system and have become an important element of the multilevel medical insurance system.

Characteristics and advantages of China's healthcare security system

[5] The Chinese government has always regarded people's health and life safety as its basic responsibility, by providing the BMI as a public good for all Chinese citizens. However, a deficit in coverage still exists between China and other countries with developed social security systems. The proportion of total medical insurance financing is about 2.5% of China's GDP, which is not high, but it is generally compatible with the per capita GDP of US $10,000 in China.

[6] Provide more. For one, government funding should be increased. From 2007 to 2019, government funding for medical security increased from CNY ￥91.3 billion CNY ￥800 billion, and the proportion of government spending on medical insurance increased from 1.87% to 3.50%. In 2020, the government subsidy for resident medical security reached CNY ￥550 per person. For another, focus should remain on the low-income population. Policies should lean towards the low-income population to ensure they have access to the BMI. The government continued to increase funding, and more than 99.9% of registered low-income citizens are now insured. The imbursement rate of hospitalization expenses has stabilized at around 80% for the low-income population after the broad coverage provided by the triple security system: the BMI, critical illness insurance, and medical aid.

[7] Stay within economic capabilities. To ensure the sustainable balance of the fund, financial overcommitment should be avoided, and the planning should be informed by the current level of economic development. The fund should meet the basic needs of people, but it should avoid becoming a welfare fund.

[8] Reinforcing the administration of the security system. First, a nationally organized volume-based procurement and use of drug standard should be established. A total of 112 types of drugs were procured by China in three batches, with the costs decreasing by an average of 54%, which saved CNY ￥53.9 billion annually. Second, the catalog of medicines covered by

the national health security system should be dynamically adjusted. Some obsolete drugs have been removed from the catalog to make room for drugs with more clinical value. Third, a reformation of medical insurance payment methods needs to be steadily implemented. In China, 97.5% of the local administrations have capped the total regional expense of medical insurance, and more than 30 pilot cities have launched diagnosis-related group payment systems. Fourth, medical organizations should be strictly supervised and unlawful practices should be heavily penalized. In the past 2 years, 330,000 unlawful organizations were suspended, and CNY ¥12.56 billion in funds were retrieved. In 2019, 69 inspection teams were sent to 30 provinces across the country to conduct unannounced field inspections, and CNY ¥2.232 billion in illegal funds were found.

Reforming the drug pricing mechanism and promoting drug availability for patients

[9] The NHSA has implemented dynamic adjustments to the catalog of medicines covered by the national health security system and issued the Interim Measures on the Administration of Medicines under the Basic Medical Insurance. The interim measures are oriented towards meeting the basic medicinal needs of citizens and ensuring that drug expenditures are compatible with BMI funding. It is necessary to ensure a scientific, standardized, precise, and dynamic management of medical insurance drugs. For exclusively produced drugs, the price is determined by catalog access negotiation, which not only saves medical insurance funds but also significantly reduces the burden of cost to patients. The establishment of a dynamic adjustment mechanism can facilitate the timely inclusion of more effective drugs into the catalog.

[10] An example of this has been in the management of hepatitis-related drugs. In recent years, with the continuous efforts of the government, the price of drugs for viral hepatitis has been reduced substantially. In 2015, the annual treatment cost of hepatitis B antiviral drugs, tenofovir disoproxil fumarate (TDF) and entecavir, was about CNY ¥20,000 and CNY ¥9,000 per person, respectively. In 2018, after the "4+7" Pilot Program was launched, the annual treatment cost of TDF and entecavir was decreased to CNY ¥210-240 per person. In 2019, after more cities were included in the pilot program, the cost of the two drugs was further decreased to CNY ¥70. After the centralized procurement of entecavir, the total procurement volume was 3.5 times lower than that of the previous year in the "4+7" pilot cities. The same year, the NHSA also negotiated and reimbursed a variety of hepatitis C oral drugs, so the out-of-pocket costs paid by patients dropped by 95%. With the substantial reduction in drug prices, the diagnosis rate and the availability of chronic hepatitis treatment were considerably improved, which enabled China to achieve the 2030 Sustainable Development Goal outlined by the World Health Organization: eliminating hepatitis as a public health threat.

Building a multilevel medical security system to reinforce support capabilities

[11] In recent years, China's commercial health insurance premium income has developed rapidly at an annual growth rate of 30%. In 2019, the premium income of commercial health insurance was CNY ¥706.6 billion, which represented a year-on-year increase of 29.7%. To meet people's growing needs of health care in the new era, the government proposes to strengthen the triple security system, which includes basic medical insurance, critical illness insurance, and medical aid, and promote various complementary medical insurance programs for major and critical diseases. The development of commercial health insurance will be accelerated, more health insurance products will be offered, the individual income tax policies for commercial health insurance will be applied in a more effective way, and the scope of insurance products will be expanded.

Seizing opportunities, meeting challenges, and promoting the high-quality development of medical security

[12] The year 2020 is the final year of 13th Five-Year Plan, and it is also the year to lay a good foundation for the 14th Five-Year Plan. Standing at this critical juncture, it is necessary to have a clear understanding of the challenges faced by health security.

[13] The demographics of the Chinese population poses serious challenges to the sustainability of the fund. The number of people over the age of 60 will exceed 300 million people at the end of the 14th Five-Year Plan, and the ratio of employees to retirees will continue to decline. Another serious challenge is that communicable diseases and chronic diseases pose a "double burden" on China's medical insurance funds. There is still a gap between the healthcare security support and the medical expectations of citizens.

[14] Medical security is highly relevant to the vital interests of the Chinese people as a whole. During the 14th Five-Year Plan period, the government will continue to promote the integrity of the multilevel medical security and guide the coordinated development of medical security, treatment, and medicine, so that the people can have more clear and accountable expectations for their health security and a greater sense of gain, healthy security and happiness in turn.

Ⅰ. Answer the following questions.

1. What is the purpose of establishing a national medical security system in China?

2. What is medical aid in China's healthcare system?

3. What should be established to reinforce the administration of the security system in China's healthcare system?

4. What are the two types of diseases that pose a "double burden" on China's medical insurance funds?

5. What is the government's goal for promoting the integrity of multilevel medical security during the 14th Five-Year Plan period?

Ⅱ. **Translate the following paragraph into English.**

中医是中华文化不可分割的一部分,为振兴华夏做出了巨大贡献。如今,中医和西医在中国的医疗保健领域并驾齐驱。中医以其独特的诊断手法、系统的治疗方式和丰富的典籍材料备受世界瞩目。中国的中医事业由国家中医药管理局负责。现在国家已经出台了管理中医的政策、法令和法规,引导并促进这个新兴产业的研究和开发。在定义上,中医是指导中国传统医药理论和实践的一种医学,它包括中草药、针灸、推拿、气功和食疗。

● Passage 2

●●● *Reform and Medical Costs* ●●●

[A] Americans are deeply concerned about the relentless rise in health care costs and health insurance premiums. They need to know if reform will help solve the problem. The answer is that no one has an easy fix for rising medical costs. The fundamental fix—reshaping how care is delivered and how doctors are paid in a wasteful, abnormal system— is likely to be achieved only through trial and error and incremental(渐进的)gains.

[B] The good news is that a bill just approved by the House and a bill approved by the Senate Finance Committee would implement or test many reforms that should help slow the rise in medical costs over the long term. As a report in *The New England Journal of Medicine* concluded, "pretty much every proposed innovation found in the health policy literature these days is contained in these measures".

[C] Medical spending, which typically rises faster than wages and the overall economy, is propelled by two things: the high prices charged for medical services in this country and the volume of unnecessary care delivered by doctors and hospitals, which often perform a lot more tests and treatments than a patient really needs.

[D] Here are some of the important proposals in the House and Senate bills to try to address those problems, and why it is hard to know how well they will work.

[E] Both bills would reduce the rate of growth in annual Medicare payments to hospitals, nursing homes and other providers by amounts comparable to the productivity savings routinely made in other industries with the help of new technologies and new ways to organize work. This proposal could save Medicare more than $100 billion over the next decade. If private plans demanded similar productivity savings from providers, and refused to let providers shift additional costs to them, the savings could be much larger. Critics say Congress will give in to lobbyists and let inefficient providers off the hook(放过). That is far less likely to happen if Congress also adopts strong "pay-go" rules requiring that any increase in payments to providers be offset by new taxes or budget cuts.

[F] The Senate Finance bill would impose an excise tax(消费税)on health insurance plans that cost more than $8,000 for an individual or $21,000 for a family. It would most likely cause insurers to redesign plans to fall beneath the threshold. Enrollees would have to pay more money for many services out of their own pockets, and that would encourage them to think twice about whether an expensive or redundant test was worth it. Economists project that most employers would shift money from expensive health benefits into wages. The House bill has no similar tax. The final legislation should.

[G] Any doctor who has wrestled with multiple forms from different insurers, or patients who have tried to understand their own parade of statements, know that simplification ought to save money. When the health insurance industry was still cooperating in reform efforts, its trade group offered to provide standardized forms for automated processing. It estimated that step would save hundreds of billions of dollars over the next decade. The bills would lock that pledge into law.

[H] The stimulus package provided money to convert the inefficient, paper-driven medical system to electronic records that can be easily viewed and transmitted. This requires open investments to help doctors convert. In time it should help restrain costs by eliminating redundant tests, preventing drug interactions, and helping doctors find the best treatments.

[I] Virtually all experts agree that the fee-for-service system—doctors are rewarded for the quantity of care rather than its quality or effectiveness— is a primary reason that the cost of care is so high. Most agree that the solution is to push doctors to accept fixed payments to care for a particular illness or for a patient's needs over a year. No one knows how to make that happen quickly. The bills in both houses would start pilot projects within Medicare. They include such measures as accountable care organizations to take charge of a patient's needs with an eye on both cost and quality, and chronic disease management to make sure the seriously ill, who are responsible for the bulk of all health care costs, are treated properly. For the most part, these experiments rely on incentive payments to get doctors to try them.

[J] Testing innovations do no good unless the good experiments are identified and expanded and the bad ones are dropped. The Senate bill would create an independent commission to monitor the pilot programs and recommend changes in Medicare's payment policies to urge providers to adopt reforms that work. The changes would have to be approved or rejected as a whole by Congress, making it hard for narrow-interest lobbies to bend lawmakers to their will.

[K] The bills in both chambers would create health insurance exchanges on which small businesses and individuals could choose from an array of private plans and possibly a public option. All the plans would have to provide standard benefit packages that would be easy to compare. To get access to millions of new customers, insurers would have a strong incentive to sell on the exchange. And the head-to-head competition might give them a strong incentive to lower their prices, perhaps by accepting slimmer profit margins or demanding better deals from providers.

[L] The final legislation might throw a public plan into the competition, but thanks to the fierce opposition of the insurance industry and Republican critics, it might not save much money. The one in the House bill would have to negotiate rates with providers, rather than using Medicare rates, as many reformers wanted.

[M] The president's stimulus package is pumping money into research to compare how well various treatments work. Is surgery, radiation or careful monitoring best for prostate(前列腺) cancer? Is the latest and most expensive cholesterol-lowering drug any better than its common competitors? The pending bills would spend additional money to accelerate this effort.

[N] Critics have charged that this sensible idea would lead to rationing of care. (That would be true only if you believed that patients should have an unrestrained right to treatments proven to be inferior.) As a result, the bills do not require, as they should, that the results of these studies be used to set payment rates in Medicare.

[O] Congress needs to find the courage to allow Medicare to pay preferentially for treatments proven to be superior. Sometimes the best treatment might be the most expensive. But overall, we suspect that spending would come down through elimination of a lot of unnecessary or even dangerous tests and treatments.

[P] The House bill would authorize the secretary of health and human services to negotiate drug prices in Medicare and Medicaid. Some authoritative analysts doubt that the secretary would get better deals than private insurers already get. We believe negotiation could work. It does in other countries.

[Q] Missing from these bills is any serious attempt to rein in malpractice costs. Malpractice awards do drive up insurance premiums for doctors in high-risk specialties, and there is some evidence that doctors engage in defensive medicine, by performing tests and treatments primarily to prove they are not negligent should they get sued.

Ⅰ. **Fast reading.**

Direction: Each statement of the following contains information given in one of the paragraphs in the above passage. Identify the paragraph from which the information is derived. You may choose a paragraph more than once. Each paragraph is marked with a letter.

1. With a tax imposed on expensive health insurance plans, most employers will likely transfer money from health expenses into wages.

2. Changes in policy would be approved or rejected as a whole so that lobbyists would find it hard to influence lawmakers.

3. It is not easy to curb the rising medical costs in America.

4. Standardization of forms for automatic processing will save a lot of medical expenses.

5. Republicans and the insurance industry are strongly opposed to the creation of a public insurance plan.

6. Conversion of paper to electronic medical records will help eliminate redundant tests and prevent drug interactions.

7. The high cost of medical services and unnecessary tests and treatments have driven up medical expenses.

8. One main factor that has driven up medical expenses is that doctors are compensated for the amount of care rather than its effect.

9. Contrary to analysts' doubts, the author believes drug prices may be lowered through negotiation.

10. Fair competition might create a strong incentive for insurers to charge less.

II. Translate the following paragraph into Chinese.

American medicine and healthcare system is a complex and multifaceted landscape characterized by both advancements in medical technology and persistent challenges in accessibility and affordability. The United States boasts world-renowned medical research institutions and hospitals that pioneer cutting-edge treatments and therapies, contributing significantly to global medical progress. However, the system is also known for its intricacies, with a mixture of public and private healthcare providers, insurance plans, and government programs leading to disparities in coverage and care. The issue of healthcare affordability remains a pressing concern, as many Americans face barriers to accessing essential medical services and medications. The ongoing debate surrounding healthcare reform reflects the nation's struggle to strike a balance between innovation, cost-effectiveness, and equitable access to quality care for all its citizens.

Cross-cultural Perspectives

Read the following paragraph and write a summary of 200 words.

Bridging the Gap: Cultural Difference Between Chinese and American Medical Systems

[1] Healthcare systems around the world are shaped by cultural, historical, and societal factors, which influence the way medical care is provided and received. When comparing the Chinese and American medical systems, it becomes evident that they are not only defined by differences in healthcare policies and practices but also deeply rooted in their respective cultural backgrounds. In this article, we will explore the cultural differences between the Chinese and American medical systems, shedding light on the unique approaches, values, and challenges faced by both nations.

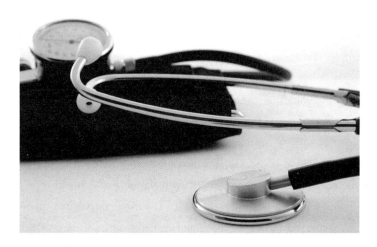

[2] Chinese culture has a rich history of traditional medicine that dates back thousands of years. Traditional Chinese Medicine (TCM) is deeply ingrained in the country's culture and is based on the principles of balance, harmony, and the flow of vital energy, or Qi. TCM

emphasizes holistic approaches, using herbal remedies, acupuncture, and various other therapies to treat illness and promote overall well-being.

[3] In contrast, the American medical system places a stronger emphasis on Western medicine, which is rooted in empirical science and the principles of evidence-based practice. While Western medicine is highly effective in treating acute conditions, it may not always address the underlying causes or provide holistic care in the same way that TCM does.

[4] Cultural differences between China and the United States are also reflected in their attitudes toward health and healthcare. China has a collectivist culture, emphasizing the importance of the family and community. In Chinese society, seeking medical care often involves input and decisions from the extended family, and individuals may feel a strong sense of obligation to prioritize their family's well-being over their own.

[5] Conversely, the United States has an individualistic culture where personal autonomy and decision-making in healthcare are highly valued. Americans are more likely to make medical decisions independently or consult with a smaller circle of close family and friends, prioritizing their individual needs and preferences.

[6] Access to healthcare is a critical aspect where cultural differences between the Chinese and American systems become apparent. In the United States, healthcare access is largely determined by insurance coverage and one's ability to pay for medical services. This individualistic approach can lead to disparities in healthcare access, as those with limited financial resources may face barriers to quality care.

[7] In China, access to healthcare is considered a social responsibility. The Chinese government has made significant efforts to expand access to medical services, especially in rural areas. The basic healthcare system in China provides essential services to the entire population, ensuring a degree of access that is not solely dependent on individual finances.

[8] The doctor-patient relationship varies considerably between China and the United States. In China, there is a strong tradition of respect for authority figures, including healthcare professionals. Patients often show deference to doctors, rarely questioning their diagnoses or treatment plans. This can sometimes lead to issues of transparency and informed consent.

[9] In the United States, the doctor-patient relationship is characterized by a more egalitarian approach. Patients are encouraged to actively participate in their healthcare decisions, ask questions, and seek second opinions. The emphasis on patient autonomy can sometimes lead to disputes and challenges in communication between patients and healthcare providers.

[10] Chinese culture places a strong emphasis on preventative healthcare. The concept of "yangsheng" or nourishing life is deeply ingrained in Chinese traditions. People often engage in practices such as tai chi, qigong, and dietary adjustments to maintain balance and prevent illness. TCM also focuses on identifying and addressing imbalances in the body before they lead to disease.

[11] In contrast, the American medical system often operates in a reactive mode, with

healthcare seeking primarily occurring in response to illness or symptoms. Preventative care is gaining recognition in the United States, but cultural differences in attitudes toward healthcare persist.

[12] Mental health is an area where cultural differences are particularly pronounced. In China, there is a significant stigma associated with mental health issues. Seeking psychological support or counseling is often viewed as a sign of weakness, and many individuals suffering from mental health problems may be hesitant to seek help.

[13] In the United States, there is a growing awareness and acceptance of mental health issues. Mental health services are widely available, and campaigns to reduce stigma have made progress in encouraging individuals to seek help when needed. The cultural differences in attitudes toward mental health can significantly impact how these issues are addressed within each society.

[14] Cultural values also play a significant role in end-of-life care decisions. In China, the concept of filial piety, or the duty to care for one's parents, is deeply ingrained. Families often face difficult decisions when it comes to withholding or withdrawing life-sustaining treatment for elderly or terminally ill relatives. The cultural emphasis on preserving life can lead to prolonged and sometimes futile medical interventions.

[15] In the United States, there is a stronger emphasis on individual autonomy and patient wishes in end-of-life decisions. Advance directives and living wills allow individuals to specify their preferences for medical treatment in advance, reducing the burden of decision-making on their families. Cultural attitudes toward death and dying influence how these ethical dilemmas are approached.

[16] While both China and the United States strive to provide quality healthcare to their populations, the cultural differences between their medical systems have a profound impact on healthcare practices, delivery, and patient experiences. Recognizing and understanding these cultural differences is essential for healthcare professionals, policymakers, and individuals in both countries. By bridging the gap and learning from each other, we can work towards more effective and culturally sensitive healthcare systems that meet the diverse needs of their populations.

◯ Case Study

The integration of Traditional Chinese Medicine (TCM) within China's modern healthcare system exemplifies the country's commitment to blending ancient traditions with contemporary medical practices.

In China, TCM has been practiced for thousands of years and is deeply embedded in the country's cultural fabric. It encompasses various modalities, including acupuncture, herbal medicine, cupping, and qigong. As China modernized, there was a concerted effort to integrate TCM into the mainstream healthcare system while maintaining its authenticity.

China's government recognized the value of TCM as a complementary approach to modern medicine. They established TCM departments within Western-style hospitals, allowing patients to access both types of treatment under one roof. Licensed TCM practitioners underwent standardized training and were included in healthcare teams, collaborating with Western-trained doctors to offer comprehensive care.

China's integration of Traditional Chinese Medicine into its modern healthcare system exemplifies the country's dedication to preserving its cultural heritage while advancing medical care. This case study demonstrates the complex process of harmonizing traditional practices with contemporary standards, providing a valuable example for other nations seeking to combine diverse medical approaches. The success of TCM integration showcases the potential for cross-cultural collaboration, innovation, and holistic patient care in an ever-evolving healthcare landscape.

Work collaboratively in groups to produce a 5-minute video illustrating your comprehension of the medicine and healthcare systems that exemplify the cultural disparities between China and America.

8-2　Unit 8 译文及答案

Unit 9

Drinks in Leisure Time

Unit Objectives

- To acquire vocabulary and expressions related to drinks in China and the West.
- To gain a general knowledge of the characteristics of drinks in China and the West.
- To express informed opinions and thoughtful analysis about drinks in leisure time.
- To develop a sense of appreciation and confidence in Chinese tea.

Read and Discuss

Read the following paragraph and discuss the following questions.

Tea originated in China and became popular around the world. The establishment of the

"International Tea Day" by the United Nations reflects the international recognition and emphasis on the value of tea. It holds great significance for revitalizing the tea industry and carrying forward tea culture. As a major producer and consumer of tea, China will work with all parties to nurture the sustained and healthy development of the global tea industry, deepen cultural exchanges surrounding tea, enable more people to understand and love tea, and share the delightful aroma and charm of tea, fostering a better life together.

1. What is the significance of the establishment of "International Tea Day" by the United Nations?
_____

2. How does China, as a major producer and consumer of tea, plan to contribute to the global tea industry's development?
_____

3. What can college students do to better present Chinese tea culture to the world?
_____

Section A

▼ Knowledge Focus

Ⅰ. Fill in the blanks based on your understanding of the online video lectures.

••• Steps of a Chinese Tea Ceremony •••

Appreciating the tea. In this step, the tea is passed around for participants to examine and admire its 1) _____.

Brewing the tea. The tea leaves are poured into the teapot. The amount of tea and water will vary with the type of tea, its quality, and the size of the teapot. Next, place the teapot into a bowl, raise the kettle at 2) _____ and pour the heated water into the teapot until it overflows. After pouring the water, 3) _____ bubbles and tea leaves on the surface and put the lid on the teapot.

9-1
Steps of a Chinese Tea Ceremony
扫码观看视频

Enjoying the fragrance of the tea. Pour the tea into the tea pitcher and fill the snifter cups with tea. Then, place the teacups upside down on top of the snifter cups, which is said to bring 4) _____. Next, the performer grabs the cups and 5) _____ them so the snifter cup is inverted into the teacup. Then the snifter cup is removed to release the tea into the teacups. The tea is usually not drunk, but poured into the bowl and 6) _____.

Refilling the teapot and steeping the tea. The teapot is then 7) _____ with fresh hot water. For oolong tea, the 8) _____ time usually ranges from 30 seconds to 10 minutes. Then, the tea is poured from the teapot into the tea pitcher; from which the tea is poured into snifter cups and then transferred to the teacups.

Tasting the tea. Good etiquette dictates that tea drinkers cradle the cup with both hands and enjoy the tea's aroma before taking a sip. One cup of tea is often drunk 9) _____. The first sip needs to be a small sip, the second sip is the largest, main sip, and the third sip is to enjoy the 10) _____. After everyone has finished the first round of tea, an unlimited number of subsequent rounds of tea can be made. The oolong tea leaves usually can be reused up to five times in a row.

Ⅱ. **Choose the best answer to each of the following questions.**

1. Who has been regarded as the "Tea Sage"?
   A. Shen Nong.
   B. Huang Di.
   C. Yuan Mei.
   D. Lu Yu.

2. If oolong tea, green tea, white tea and black tea are sequenced according to their oxidation status, which of the following is true?
   A. Oolong tea, green tea, white tea, black tea.
   B. Black tea, oolong tea, white tea, green tea.
   C. Black tea, oolong tea, green tea, white tea.
   D. Green tea, oolong tea, white tea, black tea.

3. What do people do in the production of dark tea for the convenience of transportation?
   A. The tea is steamed and pressed into bricks.
   B. The tea is slightly fermented.
   C. The tea is unfermented.
   D. The tea is fried.

4. What brought about the Chinese tea ceremony?
   A. The need to enjoy tea drinking.
   B. The requirement from the authority.
   C. The respect for nature and the need for peace.
   D. The respect for the old and the need for relaxation.

5. What are the mandatory utensils of a refined tea set?
A. A teapot, a tea strainer and teacups.
B. A tea strainer, a tea towel and teacups.
C. A teapot, a tea spoon and teacups.
D. A teapot, a tea pitcher and teacups

6. What is the appropriate temperature in making a cup of coffee?
A. 100℃.
B. 85℃.
C. 95℃.
D. 60℃.

7. What is a coffee spoon used for?
A. To mix round the coffee only.
B. To drink the coffee.
C. To mash the cube sugar.
D. To decorate.

8. Which coffee is made primarily from espresso and steamed milk?
A. Cappuccino.
B. Cafe mocha.
C. Latte.
D. Americano.

9. What was coffee once believed to be by some Christians?
A. A delicious drink.
B. The devil's drink.
C. Beverages for the poor.
D. Beverages for the rich.

10. When was coffee first developed into a hot drink?
A. During the 10th century.
B. During the 8th century.
C. During the 11th century.
D. During the 9th century.

Unit 9 Drinks in Leisure Time

Ⅲ. Decide whether each of the following statements is true (T) or false (F).

1. Tea-drinking in China can be traced back to the Tang Dynasty and rose in popularity in the Song Dynasty.

2. In China, black tea is known as crimson tea (heicha), an accurate description of the color of the liquid.

3. Before performing the tea ceremony one needs to relax and think about positive aspects of life so that the tea ceremony can be performed in a calm and relaxed manner.

4. In a Chinese tea ceremony, the first sip of tea is usually the largest, main sip to savor the flavor.

5. When brewing the tea, the amount of tea and water will vary with the type of tea, its quality, and the size of the teapot.

6. The continent of America was once the world's largest coffee producer.

7. Starbucks is seen as a groundbreaker in successfully implementing globalization and bringing a new lifestyle for the locals.

8. An authentic cappuccino is a combination of equal parts of espresso, steamed milk and hot water.

9. When drinking coffee people shouldn't drink three or four cups continuously.

10. If you want to add sugar in coffee, you can also use the sugar clamp to catch the sugar, put it besides the coffee cup and then add it in the cup.

▼ Language Focus

Ⅰ. Match the words and definitions.

____ aesthetic ____ aroma ____ beverage ____ diffuse
____ grind ____ mandatory ____ revive ____ spectacular
____ typify ____ ferment

A. to be a typical feature of something

B. any type of drink except water

C. concerned with beauty and art and the understanding of beautiful things

D. required by law

E. very impressive

F. to spread something or become spread widely in all directions

G. to become, or to make somebody/something become, conscious or healthy and strong again

H. to experience a chemical change because of the action of yeast or bacteria, often changing sugar to alcohol; to make something change in this way

I. to break or crush something into very small pieces between two hard surfaces or using a special machine

J. a pleasant, noticeable smell

II. There are 10 errors altogether in the following paragraph(s). The errors are: missing words, unnecessary words and wrong words. Please correct them as follows: for a missing word, mark its position with the symbol "∧" and write it; for an unnecessary word, cross it out with the symbol "\"; for a wrong word, underline it and write the correct word.

There are some etiquette requirements for coffee drinking. People should drink three or four cups continuously just like drinking tea or coke, and in a formal coffee cup measure is just right. Generally, drink 80-100cc is enough. Sometimes, if people want to drink continuously for three or four cups, they can add less milk or hot water. Drinking coffee before it is hot is a necessary part of tasting coffee, even in a summer. The heat of the water also play a significant role in making a cup of coffee. The appropriate temperature is 95℃. Too low temperature can't release the aroma of coffee complete and too high temperature will ruin the ingredients of coffee.	1. _____ 2. _____ 3. _____ 4. _____ 5. _____ 6. _____ 7. _____ 8. _____

Last but not least, do not drink coffee while the stomach is empty, so coffee can stimulate the gastric acid secretion, especially the gastric ulcer on which may cause health risk.

9. _____

10. _____

▼ Critical Thinking

Discuss the following questions in small groups and share your ideas in class.

1. What distinctive features characterize Chinese tea and coffee?

2. How do the cultural values embedded in tea ceremonies and coffeehouse culture influence societal norms and behaviors in China and the Western world?

3. What specific health benefits or effects are associated with the consumption of tea and coffee?

4. How might advancements in technology impact the future of Chinese tea culture and Western coffee culture?

5. What are the geographic factors contributing to the differences between Chinese tea and coffee?

6. How can individuals incorporate elements of both Chinese tea culture and Western coffee culture to create a personalized beverage experience?

▼ Case Study

Tom, an American, visited a Chinese home for the first time and was offered some tea. As he began to finish his first cup, the host added more tea to it, which surprised Tom. He proceeded to drink the second cup, but as soon as he finished it, the host continued to refill his cup for a third, fourth, and even fifth time. Tom was left feeling completely bewildered by this way of entertaining.

You are supposed to write an essay on the topic "Why was Tom totally confused?".

Section B

Passage 1

Tea Drinking in China

[A] Wherever Chinese go, the custom of drinking tea follows. Tea was first discovered by the Chinese. Tea is an indispensable part of the life of a Chinese. A Chinese saying identifies the seven basic daily necessities oil, salt, soy sauce, vinegar, and tea. The custom of drinking tea has been ingrained in the Chinese for over a thousand years. In Tang Dynasty, a man named Lu Yu created the first compendium in the world on tea, *Book of Tea*. This work helped to popularize the art of tea drinking all across China.

[B] Tea is made from the young, tender leaves of the tea tree. The differences among the many kinds of tea available are based mainly on the roasting and fermentation of the tea leaves. Through fermentation, the originally deep green leaves become reddish-brown in color. The longer the fermentation, the darker the color. Depending on the length of the roasting and degree of fermentation, the fragrance can range from floral to fruity to many.

[C] Tea is China's national drink. It contains vitamins, chlorophyll, essential oils, and fluoride. It is a diuretic capable of improving the eyesight and increasing alertness, so Chinese believe that frequent tea drinkers enjoy a longer life span. Its medical properties and benefits to the human body have actually been scientifically proven, and tea has come to be generally recognized as a natural health food.

Tea drinking customs

[D] There are several special circumstances in which tea is prepared and consumed. To show respect: In Chinese society, the younger generation always shows its respect to the older generation by offering a cup of tea. Inviting and paying for their elders to go to restaurants for tea is a traditional activity on holidays. In the past, people of lower rank served tea to higher ranking people. Today, as Chinese society becomes more liberal, sometimes at home parents may pour a cup of tea for their children, or a boss may even pour tea for subordinates at restaurants. The lower ranking person should not expect the higher rank person to serve him or her tea on formal occasions, however.

[E] For a family gathering: When sons and daughters leave home to work and get married, they may seldom visit their parents. As a result, parents may seldom meet their grandchildren.

Going to restaurants and drinking tea, therefore, becomes an important activity for family gatherings. Every Sunday, Chinese restaurants are crowded, especially when people celebrate festivals. This phenomenon reflects Chinese family values.

[F] To express thanks to your elders on one's wedding day: At the traditional Chinese marriage ceremony, both the bride and groom kneel in front of their parents and serve them tea. That is a way to express their gratitude. In front of their parents, it is a practice for the married couple to say, "Thanks for bringing us up. Now we are getting married. We owe it all to you". The parents will usually drink a small portion of the tea and then give them a red envelope, which symbolizes good luck.

Expressing gratitude for tea

[G] After a person's cup is filled, that person may knock their bent index and middle fingers (or some similar variety of finger tapping) on the table to express gratitude to the person who served the tea. Although this custom is common in southern Chinese culture such as the Cantonese, it is generally not recognized nor practiced in other parts of China. This custom is said to have originated in the Qing Dynasty when Emperor Qianlong would travel in disguise through the empire. Servants were told not to reveal their master's identity. One day in a restaurant, the Emperor, after pouring himself a cup of tea, filled a servant's cup as well. To that servant, it was a huge honor to have the Emperor pour him a cup of tea. Out of reflex he wanted to kneel and express his thanks. He could not kneel and kowtow to the Emperor since that would reveal the Emperor's identity so he bent his fingers to knock on the table to express his gratitude and respect to the emperor.

Tea wares

[H] Though not as strict as the tea ceremony in Japan, certain rules govern the Chinese understanding of tea. Take tea wares as an example. Green tea goes with white porcelain or celadon without a cover; scented tea with celadon or blue and white porcelain with a cover; black tea goes well with purple clay ware with white inside glaze, or with white porcelain or warm colored wares or coffee wares; and oolong tea is also excellent in purple clay ware. In a word, the harmonious combination of function, material, and color of tea ware is essential to brewing excellent tea. Tea wares consist of ovens, teapots, cups, tea bowls, and trays and so on. Nowadays with the development of tea procedure, we can make a cup of tea with a single porcelain cup. In the following paragraphs, we will focus on the most essential tea ware-tea cups and teapots.

[I] The custom of drinking tea propelled the development of the porcelain industry. Tang scholars preferred green porcelain from Shaoxing, Zhejiang Province. This kind of green porcelain was like crystal or jade with elegant design and exquisite decoration. Since the true color of tea was set off beautifully in this dainty cup (ou in Chinese), it was number one in Lu

Yu's Book of Tea. As to function, the size and design of the cup best suited to the tea drinking habit of that time allowed for cooking tea powder with green onion, ginger, dates, tangerine peels and mint, then drinking the whole soup.

[J] The preference for green porcelain or white porcelain was suddenly changed to black glazed teacups in the Song Dynasty. Scholars emphasized the white foam that formed when boiled water was added to the teacup. The most desirable foam was white, best presented in black tea ware. Black glazed tea ware from Fujian was dominant, while purple clay tea wares emerged in Yixing, Jiangsu. In the beginning of the Ming Dynasty, tea was made by pouring boiled water onto loose tea leaves. The tea liquor turned yellowish white, so snow-white teacups replaced the black-glazed tea ware of the Song Dynasty. In the middle of the Ming, with the advent of purple clay tea ware, focus was not limited to the color contrast of tea liquor and tea ware, but switched to the fragrance and taste of tea. The production of various teapots came to its pinnacle at the time.

[K] Tea wares made for the royal family in Jingdezhen, Jiangxi, shone brilliantly among numerous tea wares. New designs of teapots and cups increased continually with the development of tea types.

Brewing Chinese tea

[L] There are many different ways of brewing Chinese tea depending on variables like the formality of the occasion, the means of the people preparing it and the kind of tea. For example, green teas are more delicate than oolong teas or water. Being brewed, black teas should be brewed cooler.

Chaou brewing

[M] The chaou is a three-piece teaware consisting of a lid, cup/ bowl, and a saucer, which can be used on its own or with tasting cups on the side. Chaou brewing is usually employed in tea tasting situations, such as when buying tea, where neutrality in taste and ease of access to brewing leaves for viewing and sniffing is important. This method of serving is often used in informal situations, though it can also be used in slightly more formal occasions. Chaou brewing can be used for all forms of teas though lightly oxidized teas benefit most from this brewing method.

1. Boil water, or heat to specified temperature for tea, which is 80℃ for oolong tea.
2. Heat chaou with boiling water.
3. Add leaves to line bottom of chaou.
4. Rinse tea leaves and drain.
5. Slip water along the side while pouring into cup to 2/3 full.
6. Wait for 30 seconds, pour the tea.
7. Serve.

Teapot brewing

N) This is a tradition of the Minnan people and Chaozhou or Chaoshan people have made this Kungfu cha famous. Kungfu cha teapot brewing uses small Yixing purple clay teapot to "round out" the taste of the tea being brewed. Yixing teapot brewing sides towards the formal, and is used for private enjoyment of the tea as well as for welcoming guests. The following steps are one popular way to brew tea in a form widely accepted to be a kind of art. This procedure is mostly applicable to oolong teas only.

1. Boil water.
2. Rinse the teapot with hot water.
3. Fill the teapot with tea leaves up to one third of the height of the pot.
4. Rinse the tea leaves by filling the pot with hot water up to half full and draining the water immediately leaving only tea leaves behind. This step, and all subsequent steps involving pouring water, should be performed in a large bowl to catch any overflow.
5. Pour more hot water into the teapot and pour water over the teapot in the large bowl. Bubbles should not be permitted to be formed in the teapot. The infusion should not be steeped for too long: 30 seconds is an appropriate maximum.
6. Pour the first infusion into small serving cups within a minute by continuously moving the teapot around same flavor and color over the cups. Each cup of tea is expected to have the same flavor and color.
7. Pour excess tea from the first infusion, and all tea from further infusions, into a second teapot after steeping. It is possible to draw five or six good infusions from a single pot of tea, but subsequent infusions must be extended in duration to extract maximum flavor: the second infusion extended by approximately ten seconds to 40 seconds, the third extended to 45.

O) This form of the art of brewing and drinking tea is deeply appreciated by many people, including non-Chinese. Many people are enthusiastic about the art; they enjoy not only the taste of Chinese tea, but also the process of brewing it. The tea culture involved is attractive besides the relaxation it generates, allowing them to purportedly forget all the trouble in their life during the process of brewing, serving and drinking tea. Some people enjoy serving others with a cup of tea not just because they want to share their excellent tea but also their peace of mind with others.

Ⅰ. Fast reading.

Direction: Each statement of the following contains information given in one of the paragraphs in the above passage. Identify the paragraph from which the information is derived. You may choose a paragraph more than once. Each paragraph is marked with a letter.

1. The custom of knocking one's index and middle fingers on the table to express gratitude to the person who serves the tea is only common in southern Chinese culture.

2. Chinese believe that drinking tea is beneficial to their health and a longer life span.

3. The production of various teapots came to a period of prosperity because the focus of Chinese was no longer limited to the color contrast of tea liquor and tea ware.

4. In China, ways of brewing tea depend on factors like the formality of the occasion, the means of the people preparing it and the type of tea.

5. Many people are keen on the art of brewing tea because they enjoy not only the taste of Chinese tea, but also the process of brewing it.

6. For Chinese people, the function, material and color of tea ware should achieve a harmonious combination in brewing excellent tea.

7. A variety of teas differ from each other on the roasting and fermentation of tea leaves.

8. In ancient China, people of lower social status served tea to those of higher social status.

9. The custom of drinking tea has rooted in China for over one thousand years.

10. At a traditional Chinese marriage ceremony, serving the parents tea is regarded as a way to express the newlyweds' gratitude.

II. Translate the following paragraph into English.

众所周知,茶起源于中国。据说早在五六千年前,中国就有了茶树,而且有关茶树的人类文明可以追溯到两千年前。来自中国的茶和丝绸、瓷器一样,在 1000 年前为世界所知,而且一直是中国重要的出口产品。目前世界上 40 多个国家种植茶,其中亚洲国家的产量占世界总产量的 90%。其他国家的茶树都直接或间接地起源于中国。

Passage 2

What Is an Americano? Is It Different from Regular American Coffee?

[1] A longtime coffee drinker bravely stepping into a Starbucks for the first time— and completely intimidated by the menu— might figure that ordering a Caffè Americano would be a safe introduction to the world of upscale coffee. They'd quickly learn that the Americano isn't just "regular coffee" with a fancy name. In fact, it's not even drip coffee at all, even though it tastes something like the morning cup of coffee that Mabel or Sam dishes out at the local diner, or the stuff your coffee maker has waiting for you when you stumble out of bed in the morning.

[2] So what is an Americano? A Caffè Americano is espresso topped with hot water, and it can be made in several different ways. There's a good reason why this popular espresso drink has an "American name", though. To understand it, we have to go back about 80 years.

The origins of Caffè Americano

[3] Most accounts tie the creation of this coffee drink to World War II. In truth, the name may have originated even earlier; in the late 1920s, the author Somerset Maugham wrote about characters drinking an "Americano," although he never offered details on how it was made. The most credible story describing the creation and naming of Caffè Americano, however, dates back to World War II, when coffee was so important (and necessary) to the troops that the average serviceman was going through more than 32 pounds of coffee each year. The army had to grind, package and ship tons of coffee to the European theater— but often, there still wasn't enough to go around. American soldiers stationed in Italy and searching for their coffee fix supposedly hated the local espresso so much that they found a way to make it less bitter and more palatable: they diluted the espresso with hot water to make the taste more familiar. Understandably, the locals called that drink "Caffè Americano". The name, and the drink itself, stuck and grew more popular over time.

How a Caffè Americano is made

[4] Espresso and hot water sounds like a simple recipe. In reality, though, both the quality of the ingredients, and the way they're combined, will determine whether an Americano is properly prepared.

The espresso

[5] To make a great Americano, you must start with great espresso. You probably know that there's no such thing as "espresso beans". Espresso is made from the same coffee beans that are

used to make standard drip coffee. The differences are created by the roast, the blend and the brewing process.

[6] Drip coffee is brewed just as its name describes, with hot water slowly dripped through coffee grounds. When espresso is made, though, a small amount of almost-boiling water is forced through the finely-ground coffee at high pressure. The end result is a thicker, stronger, dark brown coffee which is produced in a matter of seconds, not minutes.

[7] Espresso is normally made from dark-roasted beans, because they create a fuller body and less acidity. They also create— and this is important— a thicker crema at the top. That's because of the oil that builds up on the surface of dark roast beans; it's forced out of the beans by the hot water and steam, forming an oily, rich, creamy layer of foam that rises to the top of a well-made espresso. Finally, the blend. Most coffee drinkers are aware that Arabica beans produce coffee that's cleaner, sweeter and softer, with good acidity. Robusta beans aren't usually used to make high-quality coffee, because they produce harsher coffee with more bitterness and a lot more caffeine. The exception is for espresso. Many espresso blends, particularly in America, combine Arabica beans with a small amount of Robusta beans in order to give the coffee more body and more caffeine. Mixing them isn't required; lots of people swear by espresso made from 100% Arabica beans. But Robusta beans are often used, and many aficionados who love a good espresso swear by the powerful product of the Arabica/Robusta combination. Most important of all is equipment and technique. The right espresso machine, the proper amount and distribution of grounds, and the right temperature and amount of water used to extract the brew all play huge roles in creating barista-quality espresso. To get to that point requires experience — or finding the right coffee shop.

The water

[8] Needless to say, clean, fresh water is important when making coffee. It's even more important when making an Americano, because the drink is prepared by the pour-over process; the two liquids are layered, not combined. That ensures a smoother drink and preserves the integrity of the crema. How hot should the water be? Opinions vary. Most experts shoot for 185°F, but some believe that water heated to 200°F makes a better Americano coffee. (Of course, you use cold water to make an iced Americano.) There's also a school of thought that the water has to come directly from the espresso machine, but that's purely optional.

Making the Americano

[9] We've already spoiled the surprise: a Caffè Americano isn't made by mixing espresso and hot water. The two are layered. But which goes first? The answer isn't clear-cut. Some people believe that hot water should be poured over the espresso, saying that method best preserves the espresso's body and crema. (That's the way Starbucks does it.) Others insist that the proper way to make an Americano is by pouring the espresso over the water. They claim that method creates more crema and avoids scalding the espresso if the water's too hot.

[10] Water added to espresso is known in many circles as an "original Americano". Doing it the opposite way produces what's called a "Long Black", a name coined by Australians when Italians introduced the drink Down Under.

[11] But which is "right"? We're not going to get into the middle of that argument; an Americano is great both ways. The one remaining question is how much espresso and how much water should be used. The traditional way to make a Caffè Americano is with 1-2 shots of espresso, and up to six ounces of hot water. Of course, there's no law against adding another espresso shot (or two), and many people do. For a potent Americano with extremely rich flavor, use strong espresso. If you want a less potent version, order a lungo ("long" in Italian); the ground espresso is left to extract for twice as long. That produces as much liquid as a normal double shot, but it will be weaker and may be more bitter. A better choice would be a caffè crema, a drink that's popular in Northern Italy. The extraction process is also longer than normal, but coarser-ground espresso is used to reduce the bitterness. Obviously, a double shot of espresso will have twice as much caffeine content as an Americano made with just one shot of espresso. Either way, this coffee drink is still comparable to a black coffee in that regard: 60-120 milligrams of caffeine for the Americano, about 95mg of caffeine for a cup of drip coffee.

[12] Want more caffeine? Top your Americano with a shot of black coffee. That's called a red eye.

Caffè Americano vs. other coffee drinks

[13] Usually take your coffee with milk? There's nothing wrong with adding milk to an Americano (some people call that an "Americano with milk" or a "white Americano") and most baristas will be happy to do it. An even better choice is adding steamed half-and-half. Your Americano won't quite be the same as espresso drinks like cappuccinos or lattes, though.

[14] A cappuccino is made with a shot of espresso as a base, steamed milk poured over the espresso, and a layer of steamed milk foam on top. A latte doubles the steamed milk and skips (or drastically reduces) the milk foam, with flavorings like vanilla or hazelnut often added. A macchiato is similar to a cappuccino, but with more espresso and less milk. A mocha is similar to a cappuccino, but either hot chocolate or chocolate syrup is added.

[15] You've probably noticed what's missing from all of those drinks: the hot water that's critical to making a good Americano. That doesn't mean one is better than another; after all, coffee is a matter of personal preference.

[16] To vary the basic espresso/water mix, try adding other flavor ingredients to your Americano. Flavored syrups, or spices like cinnamon, can give the classic coffee drink a different twist. To sweeten a Caffè Americano, don't mix sugar into it after it's been prepared. Instead, add sugar to the espresso and let it dissolve before adding the hot water. That will prevent the Americano from having a grainy consistency.

Can you make an Americano without an espresso machine?

[17] Sort of, but it's difficult because espresso machines and drip coffee makers use different brewing methods. Keurig makes an Americano K-cup pod; the coffee tastes good, but don't expect it to be as good as the real thing. The same goes for the Barista "Caffè Americano" ground coffee available on Amazon. You can come a little closer with a Nespresso Vertuoline machine, which is able to brew a very concentrated coffee that approaches the taste and consistency of espresso. You can also come close with a very good grinder and a French press, but that takes more work.

[18] Best bet? Try an Americano the next time you stop by Starbucks or your local high-end coffee shop. It may not turn out to be your favorite coffee drink—but you never know.

I. Answer the following questions.

1. What is generally believed about the origin of Caffè Americano?

2. Why is espresso normally made from dark-roasted beans?

3. How hot should the water be when making an Americano?

4. What is the traditional way to make a Caffè Americano?

5. What is the difference between an Americano and a cappuccino?

II. Translate the following paragraph into Chinese.

Starbucks, an international chain coffee company, is the world's best-known brand of coffee shop. It has almost 20,000 stores in around 50 countries all over the world and nearly 150,000 employees. It was founded in Seattle, Washington in 1971 by the English teacher Jerry Baldwin, the history teacher Zev Siegl and the writer Gordon Bowker. The introduction on its official website reads: "We have never changed our desire to accomplish two things every day at work: to share delicious coffee with friends and make the world a better place. That was what we expected when the first Starbucks opened in 1971, and our expectation still remains the same today." Due to a wide variety of coffee and desserts as well as its comfortable and beautiful storefront environment, the fame of Starbucks has spread throughout the world.

Cross-cultural Perspectives

Read the following paragraph and write a summary of 200 words.

The Differences and Integration between Tea Culture and Coffee Culture

[1] After thousands of years of development, tea and coffee have many differences in cultural connotation, drinking environment, internal personality and ways of thinking represented by them.

[2] Chinese tea culture originates from Chinese culture with a long history. It is broad and profound, and contains history, aesthetics, philosophy and so on. It is a peculiar cultural landscape in people's life. Whether tea producing areas or non-tea-producing areas, the creation activities and inheritance of tea culture are enduring. Chinese people like to drink tea, like its fresh and mild flavor. People who want to taste the fragrance of tea and appreciate its charm need to calm down to experience. The reason why tea can be selected and developed into a cultural phenomenon is that its pure, natural and simple character is consistent with Chinese traditional cultural values. In Chinese tea culture, tea ceremony is the core and soul. Confucianism emphasizes the golden mean of the Confucian school, benevolence and harmony, and hope people to use tea to maintain honesty; Taoism advocates nature, purity and seek quietness with tea; Buddhism emphasizes meditation and enlightenment, and uses tea to understand the principles of Zen. Chinese tea ceremony is the quintessence of oriental culture and humanistic spirit, and it is also the precious wealth inherited from 5,000 years old Chinese civilization.

[3] Compared with the implicit, elegant oriental tea culture, the western coffee culture

does not stress the complicated process. Generally speaking, it is full of passion, romance and freedom. For westerners, coffee is not only a drink, but also reflects the cultural connotation and characteristics of different countries, such as Italy's enthusiasm and innovation, Frances romantic gentleness and politeness, Germany's strict self-discipline, the United States' freedom and so on. Westerners like novelty and adventure. If they lose interest in current things, they will make other choices immediately. Therefore, coffee is closely connected with the western culture, as well as an important part of it. Furthermore, coffee culture has become the unique cultural charm of various western nationalities.

[4] Under the influence of tea culture, tea drinking has become the daily life habit of the people. For Chinese people, the environment for tea drinking is not fixed. Sometimes, they taste tea together at home when treating relatives and friends, sometimes they go to the tea house in their spare time to drink tea, and sometimes they drink a cup of tea at home alone while reading a good book in a leisurely and comfortable day. It can be seen that the purpose of Chinese drinking tea is mainly to pursue the comfort and purification of the soul. The requirements for the environment are not too high. It is enough to make the mind calm.

[5] Westerners have a strong sense of dependence on cafes, and drinking coffee has become a fixed matter in the daily life of most people. In large and small cities, there are always different kinds of cafes all over the streets. When people have a interest at any time, they will step into it and drink a cup of coffee. They can not only drink mellow coffee, but also refresh themselves. Cafe serves a main place for westerners to relax themselves. Their flourishing and prosperity symbolize westerners' positive and optimistic attitude towards life, and also means the improvement of the quality of people's material life.

[6] The traditional life style of Chinese people and the life concept of paying attention to clan and blood relationship make people form a relatively conservative personality and ignore the importance of developing culture. Tea culture reflects the conservative introversion of traditional Chinese culture. From the process of mutual introduction between tea and coffee we can see that western countries accepted tea earlier, while China began to accept coffee in the last century at a relatively slow pace. The evolution of tea taste, processing method and marketing strategy in China has also experienced a long process, but it seems that the change is not obvious for thousands of years. This can also be seen from the fact that coffee has not changed much in terms of its name and taste since it entered China. Chinese tend to respect the customs of their ancestors. This concept gradually infiltrated into the tea culture, so conservative introversion has become a representative feature of tea culture.

[7] Western countries are more affected by geography. While seeking survival, people also cultivate their spirit of exploration and innovation, and integrate this spirit into their own culture to form a unique cultural style. Western countries are much faster than China in accepting new things, so they are not satisfied with the status quo, keep moving forward, and promote the continuous development of things. In the process of mutual penetration of tea and coffee, the

differences in the development between China and the West are also obvious. For example, the West has been constantly innovating in coffee taste, types and sales methods to meet the taste needs of the public. And they can continuously develop and innovate in coffee planting and production technology. Another example is that in a relatively short period of time, Westerners have developed bagged tea which is easy to carry and brew, instant tea which can save time, hot tea which breaks the tradition, and ice tea which can relieve summer heat. Although China is still a big country of tea drinking, western countries use their own advantages to develop new ways of tea drinking. It is hoped that while maintaining its own tea culture, Chinese should strive to explore and innovate, develop new forms of tea culture, and better introduce Chinese tea to the world.

[8] In a word, behind the tea culture is a kind of related understanding thinking. Chinese tea ceremony emphasizes the unity of man and nature. Tea making goes beyond its natural attribute and becomes an important medium carrying the traditional Chinese moral ideal and spiritual realm. The Western coffee culture embodies a kind of linear thinking. Coffee, as an objective material, is scientifically and rationally understood, explored and consumed.

[9] In recent years, cross-cultural communication between China and the West has become more and more frequent, and has achieved better results. With different heritage and spirit, tea culture and coffee culture have also been closely combined. The most significant is that tea and coffee, as a bridge of cross-cultural communication, have appeared in the daily life of China and the West.

[10] In China, especially in university campuses and urban office buildings, you can often smell the aroma of coffee. It is not difficult to judge that coffee is capturing the hearts of the young generation and becoming a favorite drink for young people. A variety of cafes emerge in an endless stream, including Starbucks of the United States, Tim Hortons of Canada and other international famous brands. The younger generation in China has a higher acceptance to coffee, and generally can adapt to the feeling and taste of coffee. While drinking coffee, they can also have an in-depth exploration of western culture.

[11] In the West, the tea-houses on the street emerge as the times require. When Westerners enter the tea-houses and drink tea with elegant tea ceremony. It seems that the troubles of the world are forgotten, and there is only endless purity left. In this process, Westerners can deeply experience Chinese culture and further shorten the distance between Chinese and Western cultures. Whether in China or the West, the decoration of various tea-houses and cafes highlights the localization and provides corresponding local services. This is also the integration of tea culture and coffee culture.

[12] The two drink cultures are constantly infiltrating and integrating with each other. By drinking coffee, Chinese people absorb the enthusiastic and romantic adventure spirit of Westerners. While maintaining their own good quality, the Chinese people can move forward boldly to the future. By drinking tea, Westerners learn the gentle and modest temperament from

traditional Chinese culture and find peace of mind in the restless society. Sometimes we drink coffee but with a tea drinking attitude. The integration of tea culture and coffee culture helps Chinese and Westerners understand and learn from each other and is of great benefit to promoting the process of globalization.

Case Study

During the Cold War, when the Americans launched the Apollo Moon-landing Project, a tragic accident occurred. In the midst of uncertainty surrounding the fate of the three astronauts, the ground commander provided solace, saying "Come on! Sweet-smelling hot coffee awaits you".

If Chinese individuals were to encounter a distressing situation, would they say, "Come on! A cup of warm, fragrant tea awaits you"?

Work collaboratively in groups to produce a 5-minute video illustrating your interpretation of this phenomenon.

9-2　Unit 9 译文及答案

Unit 10
Literature

Unit Objectives

- To master words and expressions about literature in China and the West.
- To have a general knowledge on the development of literature in China and the West.
- To express opinions about literary classics.
- To develop a sense of appreciation and confidence in Chinese literature.

Read and Discuss

Read the following paragraph and discuss the following questions.

We will stay firmly rooted in Chinese culture. We will collect and refine the defining symbols and best elements of Chinese culture and showcase them to the world. We will accelerate the development of China's discourse and narrative systems, better tell China's stories, make China's voice heard, and present a China that is credible, appealing, and respectable. We will strengthen our international communications capabilities, make our communications more effective, and strive to strengthen China's voice in international affairs so it is commensurate with our composite national strength and international status. We will deepen exchanges and mutual learning with other civilizations and better present Chinese culture to the world.

1. What is the purpose of strengthening our international communication capabilities and deepening mutual learning with other civilizations?
_____

2. How does China plan to accelerate the development of its discourse and narrative systems?
_____

3. In what ways can Chinese literary works contribute to a better understanding of Chinese civilization and thought?
_____

Section A

▼ Knowledge Focus

Ⅰ. **Fill in the blanks based on your understanding of the online video lectures.**

••• *Turn of the 20th Century* •••

At the beginning of the 20th century, American novelists were expanding fiction's social spectrum to 1) _____ both high and low life and sometimes connected to the naturalist school of realism. In her stories and novels, Edith Wharton 2) _____ the upper-class society in which she had grown up. One of her finest books, *The Age of Innocence*, centers on a man who chooses to marry a conventional, socially acceptable woman rather than a 3) _____ outsider. At about the same time, Stephen Crane, best known for his Civil War novel *The Red Badge of Courage*, depicted the life of New York City prostitutes in *Maggie: A Girl of the Streets*. And in *Sister Carrie*, Theodore Dreiser 4) _____ who moves to Chicago and

10-1
Turn of the
20th Century
扫码观看视频

becomes a kept woman.

American writers also expressed the 5) _____ following upon the war. The stories and novels of F. Scott Fitzgerald capture the restless, 6) _____, defiant mood of the 1920s. Fitzgerald's characteristic theme, expressed 7) _____ in *The Great Gatsby*, is the tendency of youth's golden dreams to dissolve in failure and disappointment.

Ernest Hemingway saw 8) _____ first-hand as an ambulance driver in World War Ⅰ, and the carnage persuaded him that abstract language was mostly 9) _____. He cut out unnecessary words from his writing, simplified the sentence structure, and concentrated on concrete objects and actions. He adhered to a moral code that 10) _____, and his protagonists were strong, silent men who often dealt awkwardly with women. *The Sun Also Rises* and *A Farewell to Arms* are generally considered his best novels; in 1954, he won the Nobel Prize in Literature.

Ⅱ. Choose the best answer to each of the following questions.

1. Which of the following statements about ci is correct?

   A. The rules of prosody in ci are particularly strict.

   B. Ci was very prosperous in the Tang Dynasty.

   C. Ci originated in the Sui Dynasty.

   D. Ci has requirements for the number of words in each sentence.

2. Who is known for extensively and effectively using methodological reasoning in his polemic prose?

   A. Confucius.

   B. Zhuang Zi.

   C. Mencius.

   D. Mo Zi.

3. When did Chinese poetry reach its zenith?

   A. In Song Dynasty.

   B. In Han Dynasty.

   C. In Tang Dynasty.

   D. In Yuan Dynasty.

4. What was the main aspect presented by the author in *Romance of the Three Kingdoms*?

   A. Complex tactics.

   B. Sophisticated strategies.

   C. Patriotic activities.

   D. Weapons and warfare.

5. In which dynasty were great dramas and classic fictional novels in the vernacular language written?

  A. Tang Dynasty.

  B. Song Dynasty.

  C. Yuan Dynasty.

  D. Ming Dynasty.

6. Which of the following is NOT the characteristic of Mark Twain's works?

  A. Colloquial speech.

  B. A sense of humor.

  C. A realistic view.

  D. An idealistic view.

7. What is the main theme of *The Old Man and the Sea*?

  A. Love and Sacrifice.

  B. Suffering and Perseverance.

  C. Wealth and Power.

  D. Devotion and Loyalty.

8. Which one of the following writers did not win a Nobel Prize?

  A. Alice Walker.

  B. Ernest Hemingway.

  C. William Faulkner.

  D. Eugene O'Neil.

9. Who is regarded as the father of American literature?

  A. James Fenimore Cooper.

  B. Ralph Waldo Emerson.

  C. Thomas Jefferson.

  D. Washington Irving.

10. Which statement below best describes the meaning of Poe's works?

  A. They convey a sense of humor.

  B. They were studied at the level of human mentality.

  C. They pushed the development of fiction toward reality.

  D. They belong to Colonial Literature.

Ⅲ. **Decide whether each of the following statements is true (T) or false (F).**

1. *The Classic of History* is a collection of documents and speeches alleged to have been written by rulers and officials of the early Zhou period and before.

2. Vernacular fiction became popular after the fourteenth century, and it was esteemed in court circles.

3. Li Bai was known as a Confucian moralist; Du Fu was known for the romanticism of his poetry.

4. Sanqu, a more strict form based on dramatic arias, developed. The use of sanqu songs in drama marked an important step in the development of later novel.

5. The Song era poet Su Zhe mastered the ci, shi, and fu forms of poetry, as well as prose, calligraphy, and painting.

6. Benjamin Franklin & Jonathan Edwards are from the Colonial and Revolutionary Periods.

7. Walt Whitman was a worker, a tourist and a poetic creator.

8. Henry James is the representative of the Colonial Literature.

9. *The Scarlet Letter*, *The House of the Seven Gables*, *The Marble Faun* and *Nature* are Nathaniel Hawthorne's works.

10. Hemingway's style changed the way Americans wrote their Language.

Language Focus

Ⅰ. **Match the words and definitions.**

____ allegiance   ____ allude   ____ ingenious   ____ interrelated
____ perseverance ____ poignant ____ proponent   ____ restoration
                   ____ turbulent ____ vernacular

A. be connected and have an effect on each other

B. having a strong effect on your feelings, especially in a way that makes you feel sad

C. to mention something or someone indirectly

D. a person who supports an idea or course of action

E. a person's continued support for a political party, religion, ruler, etc.

F. having a lot of clever new ideas and good at inventing things

G. the quality of continuing to try to achieve a particular aim despite difficulties

H. the language spoken in a particular area or by a particular group, especially one that is not the official or written language

I. in which there is a lot of sudden change, confusion, disagreement and sometimes violence

J. the work of repairing and cleaning an old building, a painting, etc. so that its condition is as good as it originally was

II. There are 10 errors altogether in the following paragraph(s). The errors are: missing words, unnecessary words and wrong words. Please correct them as follows: for a missing word, mark its position with the symbol "∧" and write it; for an unnecessary word, cross it out with the symbol "\"; for a wrong word, underline it and write the correct word.

Oath in the Peach Garden is one of the iconic moment in the *Romance of the Three Kingdoms* novel. In the first chapter, Liu Bei, Guan Yu, and Zhang Fei met after they fight the Yellow Turban Rebellion and instantly befriended one another. To ensure their fraternal loyal, the three men swore brotherhood the following day. They sacrificed a black ox, a white horse, and a prepared wine. If they burned incense, they bowed their heads and cited the oath.

The Oath of the Peach Garden was an oath in the historical novel *Romance of the Three Kingdoms*, by who the three warriors Liu Bei, Guan Yu, and Zhang Fei became sweared brothers in a ceremony amid peach blossom trees. The origin goal of the Peach Garden Oath

1. _____
2. _____
3. _____
4. _____
5. _____
6. _____
7. _____
8. _____

was protect the Han Dynasty from the Yellow Turbans. This act bound the three key men of the future Shu-Han Kingdom of China and is often alluded in a symbol of fraternal loyalty.

9. _____

10. _____

● Critical Thinking

Discuss the following questions in small groups and share your ideas in class.

1. How did American literature reflect and respond to the social and cultural changes of the turn of the 20th century?

2. In what ways did Chinese literature during the turn of the 20th century differ from American literature in terms of thematic focus and approach?

3. What factors do you believe contribute to the glory of Chinese literature?

4. What impact did the Qin Dynasty have on the development of Chinese literature?

5. In the context of literature, what are the differences between how Eastern and Western cultures convey the emotions of characters?

6. In 2012, when Mo Yan was awarded the Nobel Prize in Literature, judge Goran Malmqvist highlighted that Chinese literature should have gained global recognition much earlier, but there is a scarcity of translated works in foreign languages. In your view, what are the main challenges and obstacles faced in the translation of Chinese literature?

● Case Study

Due to the shared theme of "hardship and perseverance," some individuals compare *To Live* to the Chinese equivalent of *The Old Man and the Sea*.

What is your opinion about the two books? Please write a short essay to illustrate your interpretation of the two books.

Section B

Passage 1

Modern Chinese Literature

May Fourth period

[A] Following the overthrow of the Qing Dynasty and the establishment of the republic in 1912, many young intellectuals turned their attention to the overhauling of literary traditions, beginning with the language itself. In January 1917 an article by Hu Shih, a student of philosophy at Columbia University, entitled "Wenxue gailiang chuyi" ("Tentative Proposal for Literary Reform") was published in *Xinqingnian* (*New Youth*), a radical monthly magazine published in Beijing. In it Hu called for a new national literature written not in the classical language but in the vernacular, the living "national language" (guoyu). Chen Duxiu, the editor of *Xinqingnian*, supported Hu's views in his own article "Wenxue geming lun" ("On Literary Revolution"), which emboldened Hu to hone his arguments further in a second article (1918), "Jianshe de wenxue geming lun" ("Constructive Literary Revolution"), in which he spelled out his formula for a "literary renaissance".

[B] The literary reform movement that began with these and other "calls to arms" was an important part of the larger New Culture Movement for cultural and sociopolitical reform, which was greatly strengthened by a student protest on May 4, 1919, against the intellectual performance of the Chinese delegates to the Paris Peace Conference formally terminating World War I. At the outset, the literary reformers met with impassioned but mostly futile opposition from classical literati such as the renowned translator Lin Shu, who would largely give up the battle within a few years.

[C] The first fruits of this movement were seen in 1918 and 1919 with the appearance in *Xinqingnian* of such stories as "Kuangren riji" ("The Diary of a Madman"), a Gogol-inspired piece about a "madman" who suspects that he alone is sane and the rest of the world is mad, and "Yao" ("Medicine"), both by Zhou Shuren. Known by the pseudonym Lu Xun, Zhou had studied in Japan and had become a leader of the literary revolution soon after returning to China. Lu Xun's acerbic, somewhat Westernized, and often satirical attacks on China's feudalistic traditions established him as China's foremost critic and writer. His *Ah Q Zhengzhuan* (1921, *The True Story of Ah Q*), a damning critique of early 20th-century conservatism in China, is the representative work of the May Fourth period and has become an international classic.

[D] These early writings provided the impetus for a number of youthful intellectuals to pool their resources and promote shared ideals by forming literary associations. In 1920 Shen Yanbin, better known later as Mao Dun, and others established the Wenxue Yanjiuhui (Literary Research Association), generally referred to as the "realist" or "art-for-life's-sake" school, which assumed the editorship of the established literary magazine *Xiaoshuo Yuebao* (*Short Story Monthly*). Perhaps the most important literary magazine of the early 1920s, *Xiaoshuo Yuebao* was used by the Association to promote the so-called "new literature", most major fiction writers publishing their works in it throughout the 1920s, until the magazine's headquarters was destroyed by Japanese bombs in 1932. The socially reflective, critical-realist writing that characterized this group held sway in China well into the 1940s, when it was gradually eclipsed by more didactic, propagandistic literature. Members of the smaller Chuangzao She (Creation Society), on the other hand, were followers of the "Romantic" tradition who eschewed any expressions of social responsibility by writers, referring to their work as "art for art's sake". In 1924, however, the society's leading figure, Guo Moruo, converted to Marxism, and the Creation Society evolved into China's first Marxist literary society. Much of the energy of members of both associations was expended in translating literature of other cultures, which largely replaced traditional Chinese literature as the foundation upon which the "new literature" was built. This was particularly true in drama and poetry, in which figures such as Norwegian dramatist Henrik Ibsen and Indian poet Rabindranath Tagore, respectively, were as well known to Chinese readers as indigenous playwrights and poets. In drama, the Nanguo She (South China Society), founded by Tian Han, produced and performed several short plays that were a mixture of critical realism and melodrama, while poets of the Xinyue She (Crescent Moon Society), such as the British-educated Xu Zhimo and the American-educated Wen Yiduo, were creating new forms based on Western models, introducing the beauty of music and color into their extremely popular lyrical verse.

1927-1937

[E] Political events of the mid-1920s, in which Nationalist, Communist, and warlord forces clashed frequently, initiated a shift to the left in Chinese letters, culminating in 1930 in the founding of the Zuoyi Zuojia Lianmeng (League of Left-Wing Writers), whose membership included many influential writers. Lu Xun, the prime organizer and titular head throughout the league's half decade of activities, had stopped writing fiction in late 1925 and, after moving from Beijing to Shanghai in 1927, directed most of his creative energies to translating Russian literature and writing the bitingly satirical random essays (zawen) that became his trademark. Among the many active prewar novelists, the most successful were Mao Dun, Lao She, and Ba Jin.

[F] Mao Dun was the prototypical realist. The subjects of his socially mimetic tableaux included pre-May Fourth urban intellectual circles, bankrupt rural villages, and, in perhaps his best-known work, *Ziye* (1933, *Midnight*), metropolitan Shanghai in all its financial and social chaos during the post-Depression era.

[G] Lao She, modern China's foremost humorist, whose early novels were written while he was teaching Chinese in London, was deeply influenced by traditional Chinese storytellers and the novels of Charles Dickens. His works are known for their episodic structure, racy northern dialect, vivid characterizations, and abundant humor. Yet it was left to him to write modern China's classic novel, the moving tale of the gradual degeneration of a seemingly incorruptible denizen of China's "lower depths"—*Luotuo Xiangzi* (1936, "*Camel Xiangzi*," published in English in a bowdlerized translation as *Rickshaw Boy*, 1945).

[H] Ba Jin, a prominent anarchist, was the most popular novelist of the period. A prolific writer, he is known primarily for his autobiographical novel *Jia* (1931, *The Family*), which traces the lives and varied fortunes of the three sons of a wealthy, powerful family. The book is a revealing portrait of China's oppressive patriarchal society as well as of the awakening of China's youth to the urgent need for social revolution.

[I] The 1930s also witnessed the meteoric rise of a group of novelists from Northeast China who were driven south by the Japanese annexation of their homeland in 1932. The sometimes rousing, sometimes nostalgic novels of *Xiao Jun and Xiao Hong* and the powerful short stories of *Duanmu Hongliang* became rallying cries for anti-Japanese youth as signs of impending war mounted.

[J] Poetry of the 1930s underwent a similar politicization, as more and more students returned from overseas to place their pens in the service of the "people's resistance against feudalism and imperialism". The lyrical verse of the early Crescent Moon poets was replaced by a more socially conscious poetry by the likes of Ai Qing, Tian Jian, and Zang Kejia that appealed to the readers' patriotic fervor. Others, particularly those who had at first gravitated toward the Crescent Moon Society, began striking out in various directions: notable works of those authors include the contemplative sonnets of Feng Zhi, the urbane songs of Beijing by Bian Zhilin, and the romantic verses of He Qifang. Less popular but more daring were Dai Wangshu and Li Jinfa, poets published in *Xiandai* (*Contemporary Age*), a Shanghai literary magazine. The latter wrote very sophisticated, if frequently baffling, poetry in the manner of the French Symbolists.

[K] While fiction reigned supreme in the 1930s, as the art of the short story was mastered by growing numbers of May Fourth writers and novels were coming into their own, probably the most spectacular advances were made in drama, largely through the efforts of a single playwright. Although realistic social drama written in the vernacular had made its appearance in China long before the 1930s, primarily as translations or adaptations of Western works, it did not gain a foothold on the popular stage until the arrival of Cao Yu, whose first play, *Leiyu* (1934, *Thunderstorm*), a tale of fatalism, retribution, and incestual relations among members of a rich industrialist's family, met with phenomenal success. It was followed over the next several years

Unit 10 Literature

by other critically and popularly acclaimed plays, including *Richu* (1936, *Sunrise*) and *Yuanye* (1937, *Wilderness*), all of which examined pressing social issues and universal human frailties with gripping tension and innovative dramaturgy. Political realities in future decades would force a steady decline in dramatic art, so that Cao Yu's half dozen major productions still stand as the high-water mark of modern Chinese theatre. Yet, even though movies, television, and other popular entertainments would weaken the resiliency of this literary form, it would still serve the nation as an effective propaganda medium, particularly during the war of resistance.

The war years: 1937-1949

[L] During the Sino-Japanese War (1937-1945), most writers fled to the interior, where they contributed to the war effort by writing patriotic literature under the banner of the Zhonghua Quanguo Wenyijie Kangdi Xiehui (All-China Anti-Japanese Federation of Writers and Artists), founded in 1938 and directed by Lao She. All genres were represented, including reportage (baogao wenxue), an enormously influential type of writing that was a natural outgrowth of the federation's call for writers to go to the countryside and the front lines. Literary magazines were filled with short, easily produced and adaptable plays, topical patriotic verse, and war-zone dispatches. Among the major writers who continued to produce work of high quality during this period were Ba Jin, Cao Yu, and Mao Dun. The short stories and novels that Sha Ding wrote in the late 1930s and mid-1940s also received acclaim from fellow writers. Ding Ling's fictional explorations of the female psyche and the social condition of women had caught the public's imagination in the 1920s, and in the late 1930s she established herself as the major literary figure in the communist stronghold of Yan'an.

Ⅰ. **Fast reading.**

Direction: Each statement of the following contains information given in one of the paragraphs in the above passage. Identify the paragraph from which the information is derived. You may choose a paragraph more than once. Each paragraph is marked with a letter.

1. During the May Fourth period, a lot of literary works against feudalism were published.

2. Lu Xun was famous for his satirical random essays after his stopping writing fiction.

3. "New Literature" took place of traditional Chinese literature to a large extent.

4. Lao She began his writing career while working in London.

5. The May Fourth Movement provided strong support for the New Culture Movement.

6. *Xinqingnian* approved of writing in vernacular Chinese.

7. Prior to Cao Yu, most realistic dramas in China drew inspiration from Western sources.

8. Chinese people were summoned by novels to join in social revolution.

9. Notable writers such as Cao Yu continued to produce significant works of exceptional quality during the war.

10. Numerous poets contributed to different aspects of the social revolution.

Ⅱ. **Translate the following paragraph into English.**

《三国演义》写于14世纪，是中国著名的历史小说。这部小说以三国时期的历史为基础，描写了从二世纪下半叶到三世纪下半叶魏、蜀、吴之间的战争。小说描写了近千个人物和无数的历史事件。虽然这些人物和事件大多是基于真实的历史，但是它们都不同程度地被浪漫化和戏剧化了。《三国演义》是公认的文学名著。自出版以来，这部小说吸引了一代又一代的读者，对中国文化产生了广泛而持久的影响。

Passage 2

American Fiction in the 20th Century

［1］Important movements in drama, poetry, fiction, and criticism took shape in the years before, during, and after World War Ⅰ. The eventful period that followed the war left its imprint upon books of all kinds. Literary forms of the period were extraordinarily varied, and in drama, poetry, and fiction the leading authors tended toward radical technical experiments.

［2］The little magazines that helped the growth of the poetry of the era also contributed to a development of its fiction. They printed daring or unconventional short stories and published attacks upon established writers. *The Dial* (1880-1929), *Little Review* (1914-1929), *Seven Arts* (1916-1917), and others encouraged Modernist innovation. More potent were two magazines edited by the ferociously funny journalist-critic H. L. Mencken—*The Smart Set* (editorship 1914-1923) and *American Mercury* (which he co-edited between 1924 and 1933). A powerful influence and a scathing critic of puritanism, Mencken helped launch the new fiction.

［3］Mencken's major enthusiasms included the fiction of Joseph Conrad and Theodore Dreiser, but he also promoted minor writers for their attacks on gentility, such as James Branch

Cabell, or for their revolt against the narrow, frustrated quality of life in rural communities, including Zona Gale and Ruth Suckow. The most distinguished of these writers was Sherwood Anderson. His *Winesburg, Ohio* (1919) and *The Triumph of the Egg* (1921) were collections of short stories that showed villagers suffering from all sorts of phobias and suppressions. Anderson in time wrote several novels, the best being *Poor White* (1920).

[4] In 1920 critics noticed that a new school of fiction had risen to prominence with the success of books such as F. Scott Fitzgerald's *This Side of Paradise* and Sinclair Lewis's *Main Street*, fictions that tended to be frankly psychological or modern in their unsparing portrayals of contemporary life. Novels of the 1920s were often not only lyrical and personal but also, in the despairing mood that followed World War I, apt to express the pervasive disillusionment of the postwar generation. Novels of the 1930s inclined toward radical social criticism in response to the miseries of the Great Depression, though some of the best, by writers such as Fitzgerald, William Faulkner, Henry Roth, and Nathanael West, continued to explore the Modernist vein of the previous decade.

Critics of society

[5] F. Scott Fitzgerald's *This Side of Paradise* (1920) showed the disillusionment and moral disintegration experienced by so many people in the United States after World War I. The book initiated a career of great promise that found fruition in *The Great Gatsby* (1925), a spare but poignant novel about the promise and failure of the American Dream. Fitzgerald was to live out this theme himself. Though damaged by drink and by a failing marriage, he went on to do some of his best work in the 1930s, including numerous stories and essays as well as his most ambitious novel, *Tender Is the Night* (1934). Unlike Fitzgerald, who was a lyric writer with real emotional intensity, Sinclair Lewis was best as a social critic. His onslaughts against the "village virus" (1920, *Main Street*), average businessmen (1922, *Babbitt*), materialistic scientists (1925; *Arrowsmith*), and the racially prejudiced (1947, *Kingsblood Royal*) were satirically sharp and thoroughly documented, though *Babbitt* is his only book that still stands up brilliantly at the beginning of the 21st century. Similar careful documentation, though little satire, characterized James T. Farrell's naturalistic *Studs Lonigan* trilogy (1932-1935), which described the stifling effects of growing up in a lower-middle-class family and a street-corner milieu in the Chicago of the 1920s.

[6] The ironies of racial identity dominate the stories and novels produced by writers of the Harlem Renaissance, including harsh portraits of the Black middle class in Nella Larsen's *Quicksand* (1928) and *Passing* (1929) and the powerful stories of Langston Hughes in *The Ways of White Folks* (1934), as well as the varied literary materials—poetry, fiction, and drama—collected in Jean Toomer's *Cane* (1923). Richard Wright's books, including *Uncle Tom's Children* (1938), *Native Son* (1940), and *Black Boy* (1945), were works of burning social protest, in their intensity, that dealt boldly with the plight of American Blacks in both the old

South and the Northern urban ghetto. Zora Neale Hurstons training in anthropology and folklore contributed to *Their Eyes Were Watching God* (1937), her powerful feminist novel about the all-Black Florida town in which she had grown up.

[7] A number of authors wrote proletarian novels attacking capitalist exploitation, as in several novels based on a 1929 strike in the textile mills in Gastonia, N. C., such as Fielding Burke's *Call Home the Heart* and Grace Lumpkin's *To Make My Bread* (both 1932). Other notable proletarian novels included Jack Conroy's *The Disinherited* (1933), Robert Cantwell's *The Land of Plenty* (1934), and Albert Halper's *Union Square* (1933), *The Foundry* (1934), and *The Chute* (1937), as well as some grim evocations of the drifters and "bottom dogs" of the Depression era, such as Edward Anderson's *Hungry Men* and Tom Kromer's *Waiting for Nothing* (both 1935). The radical movement, combined with a nascent feminism, encouraged the talent of several politically committed women writers whose work was rediscovered later; they included Tillie Olsen, Meridel Le Sueur, and Josephine Herbst.

[8] Particularly admired as a protest writer was John Dos Passos, who first attracted attention with an anti-World War I novel, *Three Soldiers* (1921). His most sweeping indictments of the modern social and economic system, *Manhattan Transfer* (1925) and the *U. S. A.* trilogy (*The 42nd Parallel*, 1919) and *The Big Money* (1930-1936), employed various narrative innovations such as the "camera eye" and "newsreel", along with a large cast of characters, to attack society from the left. Nathanael West's novels, including *Miss Lonelyhearts* (1933), *A Cool Million* (1934), and *The Day of the Locust* (1939), used black comedy to create a bitter vision of an inhuman and brutal world and its depressing effects on his sensitive but ineffectual protagonists. West evoked the tawdry but rich materials of mass culture and popular fantasy to mock the pathos of the American Dream, a frequent target during the Depression years.

Hemingway, Faulkner, and Steinbeck

[9] Three authors whose writings showed a shift from disillusionment were Ernest Hemingway, William Faulkner, and John Steinbeck. Hemingway's early short stories and his first novels, *The Sun Also Rises* (1926) and *A Farewell to Arms* (1929), were full of the existential disillusionment of the Lost Generation expatriates. The Spanish Civil War, however, led him to espouse the possibility of collective action to solve social problems, and his less-effective novels, including *To Have and Have Not* (1937) and *For Whom the Bell Tolls* (1940), embodied this new belief. He regained some of his form in *The Old Man and the Sea* (1952) and his posthumously published memoir of Paris between the wars, *A Moveable Feast* (1964). Hemingway's writing was influenced by his background in journalism and by the spare manner and flat sentence rhythms of Gertrude Stein, his Paris friend and a pioneer Modernist, especially in such works of hers as *Three Lives* (1909). His own great impact on other writers came from his deceptively simple, stripped-down prose, full of unspoken implication, and from his tough but

vulnerable masculinity, which created a myth that imprisoned the author and haunted the World War Ⅱ generation.

[10] Hemingway's great rival as a stylist and mythmaker was William Faulkner, whose writing was as baroque as Hemingway's was spare. Influenced by Sherwood Anderson, Herman Melville, and especially James Joyce, Faulkner combined stream-of-consciousness techniques with rich social history. Works such as *The Sound and the Fury* (1929), *As I Lay Dying* (1930), *Light in August* (1932), *Absalom, Absalom*! (1936), and *The Hamlet* (1940) were parts of the unfolding history of Yoknapatawpha County, a mythical Mississippi community, which depicted the transformation and the decadence of the South. Faulkner's work was dominated by a sense of guilt going back to the American Civil War and the appropriation of Indian lands. Though often comic, his work pictured the disintegration of the leading families and, in later books such as *Go Down, Moses* (1942) and *Intruder in the Dust* (1948), showed a growing concern with the troubled role of race in Southern life.

[11] Steinbeck's career, marked by uneven achievements, began with a historical novel, *Cup of Gold* (1929), in which he voiced a distrust of society and glorified the anarchistic individualist typical of the rebellious 1920s. He showed his affinity for colorful outcasts, such as the *paisanos* of the Monterey area, in the short novels *Tortilla Flat* (1935), *Of Mice and Men* (1937), and *Cannery Row* (1945). His best books were inspired by the social struggles of migrant farm workers during the Great Depression, including the simply written but ambiguous strike novel *In Dubious Battle* (1936) and his masterpiece, *The Grapes of Wrath* (1939). The latter, a protest novel punctuated by prose-poem interludes, tells the story of the migration of the Joads, an Oklahoma Dust Bowl family, to California. During their almost biblical journey, they learn the necessity for collective action among the poor and downtrodden to prevent them from being destroyed individually.

Ⅰ. **Answer the following questions.**

1. What are some valuable insights we can gain from *The Great Gatsby*?

2. Why does the author describe Richard Wright's books as works of passionate social protest?

3. What can we learn about John Dos Passos?

4. How to understand Hemingway's impact on other writers?

5. What is the main story that *The Grapes of Wrath* conveys to readers?

Ⅱ. **Translate the following paragraph into Chinese.**

The sister, Catherine, was a slender, worldly girl of about thirty, with a solid, sticky bob of red hair, and a complexion powdered milky white. Her eyebrows had been plucked and then drawn on again at a more rakish angle but the efforts of nature towards the restoration of the old alignment gave a blurred air to her face. When she moved about there was an incessant clicking as innumerable pottery bracelets jingled up and down upon her arms. She came in with such a proprietary haste, and looked around so possessively at the furniture that I wondered if she lived here. But when I asked her she laughed immoderately, repeated my question aloud, and told me she lived with a girl friend at an hotel. (*The Great Gatsby*)

Cross-cultural Perspectives

Read the following paragraph and write a summary of 200 words.

The Significance of Foreign Literature Translation to Cross-Cultural Communication

The transformation of language medium by translation

[1] Although foreign literature translation is the text translation based on foreign literature, it is the re-creation and translator's re-comprehension on the literature works rather than the direct presentation of foreign literature. In literary translation, people prefer to see creation. Literary translation is not a simple text translation, but a comprehension and innovation of the original text from the aspect of creation. In literary translation, fans of the original works will have a meticulous pursuit of literature, even can not tolerate any "betrayal". "Betrayal" means that during the translation of foreign literary works, the style of the works is lost, or the charm of the works disappears, which caused that the emotions of the original works can not be expressed well. During the process of translating literary works, it becomes the focus of many translators to reorganize the original text and translate the work to ensure the localization of literature without losing the originality of the work.

[2] Words are the basis of literary works. Through the expression of words, the value and connotation of the whole works can be expressed. In the process of literary translation, translators not only need to accurately translate the text, but also to recreate the written language so as to avoid the boring situation of words and languages. Translation is not only the re-creation of language, but also a means to make two languages closer. The translation of foreign documents is

the important carrier of cross-cultural communication. Translation enables people to have a deeper understanding of foreign culture and they can also understand the culture and spirit of the country and nation through works. Therefore, in the process of translation, it is necessary to understand the cultural symbols of foreign countries and to be familiar with the syntactic structure of the language so as to avoid literal translation. In fact, cross-culture is the difference of ideas and contexts to a great extent. It is not easy for translators to clear these barriers and make foreign cultures communicate and spread more smoothly in their own countries. Foreign literature translation plays a positive role and promotes the progress of civilization when foreign culture is spreading in China.

Update of citation dictionary

[3] Excellent foreign literature with rich connotation value has become the treasure of all mankind. As a spiritual food, it plays an irreplaceable role in the progress of global human civilization. The translation of foreign literature is not a simple task, but a process of recreating and processing foreign advanced literature and art, so that foreign literary works can appear in front of people's eyes. In order to play the maximum value of human spiritual wealth, it needs to be shared. Therefore, foreign literature translation is a beneficial project, which can provide help for the progress of human civilization and cross-cultural communication of literature, and make it effective in literary translation as the bridge and link.

[4] When foreign images, allusions, characters and others enter into the culture of other countries through literary translation, it is unknown what kind of sparks and chemical reactions will be produced. Many people want to know what our own culture looks like when it enters into other cultures. In fact, for a long time, the introduction of foreign literary translation, images, allusions, characters and others has enriched and replenished the citation dictionary, which has provided a lot of materials for China's literary creation and laid a solid foundation for the

progress and innovation of China's literature and art. Cross-cultural communication needs a platform and foundation, and foreign literature translation provides the possibility to consolidate this foundation. People of different countries and nationalities firstly get to know each other through literary works before they communicate with each other. Therefore, foreign literature translation is of great significance to the updating of citation dictionary.

Extradition of cultural experience

[5] In fact, we mainly learn about the world from literature and art, which is also a window for other countries and nations to understand the world. Foreign literature translation translates foreign documents into native characters, so that native people can see the private house mode, cultural value, history and religion of foreign countries. Through such a cultural display, people can realize the transmission and exchange of culture, and it is also an important way for a nation to enter into the world culture and carry forward its own culture. Only on the basis of understanding the background and basis of foreign culture, we can make our own culture go to the world better. Literature is the carrier of culture, and in the process of understanding other nationalities, literary works are the important way and window.

[6] For example, the spread of Chinese traditional culture in the west is achieved through literary translation. The Taoist aesthetic principle of "viewing things from objects" is the westerners' understanding of Taoism or traditional Chinese culture, which is indirectly understood by the translation of literature translators. When they see the Chinese literary works which are translated by translators, they will have a general understanding of Chinese culture and art. However, the translation of Chinese literature has some difficulties, especially the poetic and artistic conception of literary works, and the philosophy hidden in the text also makes the translation more difficult. Therefore, during the period of literary translation, translators should have a high literary quality and translate works in a perceptual point of view, so as to achieve the extradition effect of cultural experience.

Providing new spiritual resources for the native culture

[7] It is not advisable to create literary creation without considering the practical situation, it is also impossible to achieve the prosperity of our national culture without communication with other countries. Through literary translation, a large number of foreign excellent works can be introduced into China, which can provide spiritual resources and inspiration for the national literature creation. During the May 4th Movement of China, people's ideas were relatively free and romanticism prevailed at that time, which gave birth to a large number of romantic poems, such as "A Doll's House", which describes a new youth, Nora. She is a teacher who is emancipated in mind and dares to pursue freedom. In the 1980s, a large number of works appeared after Reform and Opening up, and many writers began to talk about the influence of foreign literature on themselves. In fact, for a country and a nation, the entry of excellent foreign

literature is a blessing. It is the influence of foreign literature translation that makes the works that can enlighten people's thoughts begin to spread in our country, and more people can change their thinking under the influence of works, and open their closed minds so that culture can be continuously supplied to the brain just like blood. In the process of cultural exchange with the world, China has become more open and goes to the world with a new mentality. It is no longer like a small family with a closed door and has no understanding of the world.

Promoting the modernization of traditional culture

[8] What a nation owns should be shared with the world. In foreign literary translation works, local culture or national culture can draw spiritual resources from it to provide support for the prosperity of knowledge and culture. In the process of going to the world and modernization, the traditional culture of our nation needs a remolding of culture and thought, and we also need to re-examine the status of our national culture in China and the world. Therefore, in the process of the development of national culture and the prosperity and diversification of local culture, we also need to actively absorb the beneficial elements of foreign literary works in the context of cultural globalization. In fact, foreign literary translation, to a great extent, will bring advanced ideas and thoughts. When readers read the translated literary works, it is a process of ideological enlightenment or self-improvement. In China's long-term development process, Chinese culture plays an important role, and the reason why Chinese culture has been prosperous for a long time is that we are inclusive and take the advantages of a hundred schools to help realize the Chinese dream in the long-term development process.

[9] How can Chinese traditional culture play a positive role in the realization of the China Dream in modern times? One of the most important methods is to learn from foreign literary works. Through the exchange with global culture, the charm of Chinese culture can be better burst out, which can not only realize the modernization of Chinese traditional culture, but also promote the pace of Chinese traditional culture to the world. In fact, how to show vitality and realize modernization of our national culture is a comprehensive problem. However, the study and absorption of foreign culture is an important way. We should actively promote our national culture to the world and to the modernization through foreign literature translation.

▼ Case Study

Many scholars have translated the famous Chinese poem "Jing Ye Si" into English, offering various versions. Which of the following version do you like best, and why?

Work collaboratively in groups to produce a 5-minute video illustrating your comprehension of features that exemplify the cultural disparities between Eastern and Western literature.

静夜思

李白

床前明月光，
疑是地上霜。
举头望明月，
低头思故乡。

Version 1:

Nightly Thoughts

Li Bai

许景城 译

Ere my bed moonlights mound,
like rime on the ground.
Head up, the moon bright,
head down, homesick I'm found!

Version 2:

Thoughts on a Tranquil Night

Li Bai

许渊冲 译

Before my bed a pool of light —
Can it be hoar-frost on the ground?
Looking up, I find the moon bright;
Bowing, in homesickness I'm drowned.

Version 3:

Thoughts in the Silent Night

Li Bai

杨宪益、戴乃迭 译

Beside my bed a pool of light —
Is it hoarfrost on the ground?

I lift my eyes and see the moon,
I bend my head and think of home.

Version 4:

Still Night Thoughts

Burton Watson 译

Moonlight in front of my bed —
I took it for frost on the ground!
I lift my eyes to watch the mountain moon,
lower them and dream of home.

Version 5:

Night Thoughts

John Turner 译

As by my bed the moon did beam,
It seemed as if with frost the earth were spread.
But soft I raise my head,
to gaze at the fair moon.
And now,
With head bent low,
Of home I dream.

10-2　Unit 10 译文及答案

参考文献 / Reference

[1] 常俊跃,霍跃红,王焱,等. 中国文化(英文版)[M]. 2版. 北京:北京大学出版社,2016.

[2] 常俊跃,李莉莉,赵永青. 美国社会与文化[M]. 北京:北京大学出版社,2018.

[3] 陈波. 中国饮食文化[M]. 北京:电子工业出版社,2016.

[4] 陈麦克. 论中美教育[M]. 海口:海南出版社,2016.

[5] 戴炜栋. 美国文化与社会[M]. 上海:上海外语教育出版社,2018.

[6] 杜莉. 中国饮食文化[M]. 北京:中国轻工业出版社,2012.

[7] 多丽丝·普瑟,张玲. 商务礼仪[M]. 北京:科学出版社,2017.

[8] 弗·司各特·菲茨杰拉德. 了不起的盖茨比[M]. 上海:上海译文出版社,2009.

[9] 弗·司各特·菲茨杰拉德. 伟大的盖茨比(英文全本)[M]. 北京:世界图书出版公司,2017.

[10] 何其莘. 美国社会与文化[M]. 北京:中国人民大学出版社,2012.

[11] 何晓明. 中国文化概论[M]. 北京:首都经济贸易大学出版社出版,2019.

[12] 黄蕙萍,单元媛,魏龙. 中国商务文化沟通[M]. 武汉:武汉理工大学出版社,2007

[13] 廖华英. 中国文化概况[M]. 北京:外语教学与研究出版社,2015.

[14] 李建中. 中国文化概论[M]. 武汉:武汉大学出版社出版,2014.

[15] 刘重霄. 中美教育、文化的体验式比较研究.[M]北京:首都经济贸易大学出版社,2020.

[16] 刘春芳. 中西文化对比教程[M]. 北京:中国人民大学出版社,2017.

[17] 刘泓,浩瀚. 用英语说中国(风俗民情)[M]. 北京:科学技术文献出版社,2008.

[18] 卢红. 中国商务文化[M]. 北京:华语教学出版社,2018.

[19] 玛格丽特·维萨. 餐桌礼仪[M]. 北京:新星出版社,2007.

[20] 马建鹰. 中国饮食文化世[M]. 上海:复旦大学出版社,2018.

［21］ 梅仁毅. 英语国家社会与文化[M]. 北京:外语教学与研究出版社,2017.

［22］ 施建蓉,周恩. 中医英语[M]. 上海:上海科学技术出版社,2020.

［23］ 王守宏,李楠. 中美文化透视与思辨[M]. 上海:复旦大学出版社,2018.

［24］ 王焱,赵牟丹. 中西文化对比教程[M]. 北京:清华大学出版社,2017.

［25］ 王志茹,陆小丽. 英语畅谈中国文化[M]. 北京:外语教学与研究出版社,2017.

［26］ 吴澍. 中国饮食文化［M］. 北京:化学工业出版社,2020.

［27］ 谢定源. 中国饮食文化［M］. 杭州:浙江大学出版社,2018.

［28］ 叶嘉莹. 叶嘉莹说初盛唐诗[M]. 北京:中华书局,2108.

［29］ 张岱年,方克立. 中国文化概论[M]. 北京:北京师范大学出版社,2020.

［30］ 张桂萍. 跨文化交际:中英文化对比[M]. 北京:外语教学与研究出版社,2019.

与本书配套的二维码资源使用说明

　　本书部分课程及与纸质教材配套数字资源以二维码链接的形式呈现。利用手机微信扫码成功后提示微信登录，授权后进入注册页面，填写注册信息。按照提示输入手机号码，点击获取手机验证码，稍等片刻收到4位数的验证码短信，在提示位置输入验证码成功，再设置密码，选择相应专业，点击"立即注册"，注册成功。(若手机已经注册，则在"注册"页面底部选择"已有账号？立即注册"，进入"账号绑定"页面，直接输入手机号和密码登录。)接着提示输入学习码，需刮开教材封面防伪涂层，输入13位学习码(正版图书拥有的一次性使用学习码)，输入正确后提示绑定成功，即可查看二维码数字资源。手机第一次登录查看资源成功以后，再次使用二维码资源时，只需在微信端扫码即可登录进入查看。